Gilles de Rais:
The Original Bluebeard

By *A. L.* VINCENT & *CLARE* BINNS

Introduction by
M. HAMBLIN SMITH, M.A., M.D.
Medical Officer of H.M. Prison, Birmingham

LONDON: A. M. PHILPOT, LTD.
69 GREAT RUSSELL STREET, W.C.1
1926

Printed in Great Britain.

GILLES DE RAIS
From a portrait by Ferron in the Versailles Gallery.

CONTENTS

Chapter		Page
	Introduction	7
I.	Early Youth of Gilles de Rais	37
II.	War and Marriage	44
III.	The Eaglet	53
IV.	Gilles and Saint Joan	67
V.	Æsthete and Murderer	81
VI.	Actor-Manager-Producer	95
VII.	Ruin	109
VIII.	Black Magic	123
IX.	The Beast of Extermination	138
X.	Gilles' Arrest	151
XI.	The Trial	163
XII.	The End	184
Appendix I.		199
Appendix II.		203
Appendix III.		208
Appendix IV.		210
Appendix V.		215
Appendix VI.		217

LIST OF ILLUSTRATIONS

GILLES DE RAIS, from a portrait by Ferron *Frontispiece*

THE CHÂTEAU OF TIFFAUGES AT THE PRESENT DAY - - - - - *Facing page* 54

GILLES DE RAIS, from a portrait by Montfaucon - - - - - ,, ,, 72

TOWER AND MOAT, CHÂTEAU OF TIFFAUGES ,, ,, 124

CRYPT OF THE CHAPEL OF ST. VINCENT, CHÂTEAU OF TIFFAUGES - - - - ,, ,, 138

CHAPEL OF ST. VINCENT, CHÂTEAU OF TIFFAUGES, AT THE PRESENT DAY - ,, ,, 158

EXECUTION OF GILLES DE RAIS - - ,, ,, 186

INTRODUCTION

THIS book presents to its readers, whose first feeling may be one of horror, but who will speedily find blending with it a sense of fascination, a study of one of the most astounding personalities of which history holds record—Gilles de Rais, the original, it is supposed, of "Bluebeard," but an infinitely more splendid and subtle wrongdoer than that legendary personage. It brings before us, with a wealth of curious and often shocking detail, Gilles de Rais as an aristocrat, as a soldier, as an epicure in perverted sensation; a man of genius, of immense wealth, of furious inverted lusts; one who did wrong more recklessly and cruelly than perhaps any Roman emperor of the Decadence, or any Italian nobleman of the Renaissance, but who did wrong with all his imagination, and with an almost superhuman energy. It is impossible to relegate such a man to the ranks of ordinary criminals. He must be studied as an artist, in some respects the supreme artist, in evil. But he should be studied, as should all offenders, in a scientific spirit, and with the object of attaining some comprehension of his actions.

To attempt the estimation, from the available evidence, of the character of remarkable historical personages, and the assessment of the causes of their actions, and their " responsibility " for those actions, has long been a favourite task with historians. Until quite recent times, however, the result of such inquiries was comparatively futile. For it is only quite lately that some of the hidden springs of human conduct have been laid bare. The light upon our path, the knowledge of the infinite complexity of human conduct, has come from the researches of many workers, and especially from those of Sigmund Freud. His hypothesis of the unconscious mind has enabled us to comprehend how and why men have acted in a way which seemed quite extraordinary to our forefathers, a way which in mediæval times gave rise to the idea of demoniacal possession. In order to understand the character and the actions of any man, we now know that we have to go much further back in his life history than was considered, at one time, to be either necessary or possible. No historical research can, of course, ever completely elucidate these cases of the past; there are many most essential details which could only be ascertained by direct personal mental analysis, and this cannot be had. Still, by interpretation of the available data, we can do far more than was formerly possible in this way. The gathering of the data is the task of the historian. The interpretation of the data appertains to the task of the psychologist.

The first duty of the psychologist, in such a case, is to decide upon what data he is going to base his interpretation of the character and the actions of his subject. In my present attempt to give a short summary of the chief points of psychological interest in the life of Gilles de Rais, I am accepting the data gathered by the authors of this book. They have had access to many hitherto unexamined documents, and have carefully considered all the historical evidence relating to the character with which they are dealing. We have thus been put into the possession of much new information concerning one of the most remarkable characters of the Middle Ages. The object of this introduction is to review the evidence in the light thrown upon it by modern psychology. The reader will then be able to comprehend something of the causative factors of Gilles' conduct, and will no longer have to regard it as an inexplicable mystery.

This book, however, is not addressed solely, or even mainly, to readers who are versed in the theories of modern psychology. It has a more general appeal. It is intended to interest all who are disposed to consider a criminological problem, and to examine the case of a highly anti-social person, not in any spirit of blame, but with the idea of finding some scientific explanation of his conduct, and of understanding the circumstances which made him what he was. It seems, therefore, necessary that the ordinary reader may have some comprehension of the attitude which is taken by modern psychology to crime, as also to other varieties of human conduct, to give a short summary of the modern theories as to mental processes (especially those of the unconscious mind) and of the development of the personality. My summary is necessarily condensed, and is, so far, unsatisfactory. But I venture to think that, so far as it goes, it is accurate, or, at least, that my statements would be accepted by most modern authorities on psychology.

The basis of the mind—and in using the term "basis" I am, of course, only speaking figuratively—consists of a number of primitive instincts. These instincts are situated in the unconscious mind, and from them springs all the psychic energy which we make use of in our daily lives. It is not necessary for our purpose to enter into the controversies as to the relative importance of these various instincts. But, in speaking of the sex instinct, we must remember that the term "sex," when used in the Freudian sense, includes much more than we have been wont to place under that head. Under the conditions of modern, and even of mediæval civilisation, the sex instinct is more thwarted and repressed than is any other.

But the contents of the unconscious mind are not formed in this way alone. Certain experiences or wishes may be so completely at variance with the mind as a whole that what is known as a mental conflict occurs, and the offending complex (this being the name given to a system of ideas with a strong emotional tone, and a tendency to produce actions of a definite character) is, or may be, repressed into the unconscious. But it is not thereby destroyed, or merely stored away. It is constantly trying to make its escape into consciousness. And it may so escape in various ways, and may occasion conduct of every imaginable kind.

These facts are now accepted by practically all modern psychologists. And it is clear that they throw an entirely new light upon the causative factors of human conduct, whether criminal or not.

Gilles de Rais was a homo-sexual, a sexual invert. To understand the view which modern science takes of this condition, it is necessary to give some attention to the development of the personality. The normal personality passes through several distinct stages. Starting with the birth of the child, Freud holds that there is a constant conflict between what he terms the Pleasure-principle, which is supreme in inter-uterine life, and the Reality-principle. Freud also holds that elements of sexuality exist from birth. The first stage, that of infancy, is a time when all the child's desires tend to be satisfied by the mother, or her surrogate, and the sexuality at this stage may well be termed incestuous. Then comes a stage which is characterised by the formation of what is termed the Ego-estimate, a stage at which the dominant form of sexuality is termed narcissistic. The child begins to resent the exercise of authority by others, and gives indications of a complex on this subject. We next have a stage in which the prevailing fantasy, at least in boys, is that of belonging to a team, and the type of sexuality is definitely homo-sexual, and is directed to individuals of the same sex. In normal cases this stage merges, at puberty, into the ordinary hetero-sexual stage, with direction to individuals of the opposite sex. But development does not always proceed normally, and we may get a fixation at any stage, with resulting conduct which will be looked upon with disfavour by ordinary individuals. As personality develops, the characteristics of the preceding stages are repressed, but are not destroyed. On account of the attitude of society, the types of sexuality characteristic of the earlier stages are repressed, and are replaced in consciousness by their opposites. But the repressed elements persist in the unconscious mind and have their effect upon the development of personality.

Homo-sexuality, or sexual inversion, is a condition in which the person is attracted by members of the same sex as himself, and has not the normal attraction towards members of the opposite sex. It is, as we have just seen, a fixation at an earlier, a prepubertal stage in development. The condition is far more common than is generally known, and occurs in women at least as frequently as in men. Homo-sexuality is looked upon with great disfavour by society. It is not necessary for us to enter into the reason for this disapproval. Probably the biological uselessness of homo-sexuality is at the basis of society's disapprobation. The fact of this disapprobation is well known to homo-sexuals, on account of their early training. As a result, the sense of inferiority, the inferiority complex, which is present in all personalities,

Introduction

and is due to the constant conflict between the self-assertive and the submissive tendencies, is increased. To this homo-sexuals react in one of two ways, either by concealment of their tendency, or by an attempt to justify it. Justification is, however, quite futile. Society is entitled to determine what shall be its attitude to homo-sexuality, as to all other forms of conduct. The disapproval of society exists, and it has to be faced. Still, the fact remains that there is, probably, a certain element of homo-sexuality, although it may be but a small one, present in every personality. The origin of the more marked forms of homo-sexuality is probably to be found in the way in which the subject regards his own parents. If by undue dependence, or in some other way, a child identifies himself or herself with the parent of opposite sex, he or she becomes a homo-sexual.

Gilles was not only a homo-sexual, he was

also a sadist. It is necessary to say a few words upon this abnormality. Sadism is a condition in which the sex instinct is gratified and stimulated by the infliction of pain or cruelty on others. It is not always necessary that the pain should be inflicted personally; it may be enough to see the pain inflicted by another, or even to read or hear of its infliction. This is the explanation of the delight which many, perhaps most boys, take in the reading of stories of executions and tortures. And it is likely that, as with homosexuality, there is a sadist element in every personality. But sadism, in its full manifestation, is only gratified by the personal infliction of the pain. It is not always necessary that the victim should be a human being; there are instances on record of the sadistic killing of animals. The connection with the sacrificial immolation of victims will be noticed. Sadism is very common in the animal kingdom. In man there is reason to believe that the condition arises from aggressiveness in childhood, perhaps arising as a defence reaction to feelings of inferiority. The aggressiveness may take the form of an ardent desire to obtain knowledge on sex matters.

Having thus briefly reviewed certain leading features in the theories of modern psychology, we are in a position to trace the gradual development of Gilles de Rais' personality, and to see how the various events of his life combined to make him what he was.

Gilles was born during the period in which France was distracted by the fighting between the various factions in the Hundred Years' War, a fact which will have to be remembered when we come to consider how it was that his misdeeds were allowed to go on so long. His father was a noble of great wealth and power, and Gilles' resulting social position also had its effect. The father died when Gilles was nine years of age, but this time would fully suffice for the establishment of a strong father complex, an attitude of antagonism to the position and the authority of the father. Gilles' mother soon married again, and this would be a very disturbing factor in the boy's life. He and his younger brother were brought up by their maternal grandfather, to whose authority the antagonism to the father would be transferred, probably with accentuation. The younger brother was the guardian's favourite; and it is likely that, as the younger child, he would have been the mother's favourite, and perhaps also that of the father. A strong complex would be induced in Gilles' mind by these factors. We learn that he drifted into a habit of solitude. It is not impossible that he may have been near that type of insanity known as *dementia præcox*, of which a tendency to solitude is often a marked feature. His solitary propensities would be increased by the fact that living in a country where, and at a time when, communications were difficult, there was no one with whom he would have been allowed to associate upon terms which at all approached equality. The adulation which he doubtless received from his servitors, together with his consciousness of being heir to vast wealth and importance, increased his egotism.

At an early age, events occurred which could not fail to produce a great effect upon his character. He was twice betrothed, first at the age of fourteen years, and again a year later. The sexuality of a boy of that age would be vastly stirred, even by the suggestion of such an event, not to speak of the stimulating effect of the betrothal ceremony, which was conducted with great impressiveness, and which had, practically, the binding effect of a marriage, though consummation did not, as a rule, follow immediately. Such would be the effect even to-day, and boys married much earlier in the fifteenth century than is now common. Gilles himself was actually married at the age of sixteen. Many a modern lad has indulged in the fantasy of the marriage relation, often of the marriage ceremony, at a much earlier age than that of fourteen years, although present-day custom obliges him to conceal this fantasy, on account of the ridicule to which he would be subjected for it. In the case of either of these betrothals, there was a marked disappointment, for both Gilles' intended brides died before the marriage was completed. These events must have had a very serious effect upon his mental life. There had been no feminine influence, and probably no feminine companionship, since the re-marriage of his mother. And the absence of means for self-expression forced Gilles into a world of fantasy, relieved only by field sports, and fed by study. Among other works he studied the lives of the Roman emperors, as related by Suetonius. All who are acquainted with the sex-stimulating effect of the tales of classical mythology, episodes which are, oddly enough, selected by the most puritanical authorities as being suitable reading for schoolboys, will appreciate the influence of this. Still more marked would be the effect of a book which dealt with the cruelties and the despotisms of the Cæsars. And Gilles himself confessed, later, how great had been the effect upon him of the tales of these emperors' sadistic cruelties to boys.

Gilles was, in many ways, a genius, and appears to have been conscious of that fact. From lack of anyone to understand him, he lived in a world of fantasy, and it is not surprising to learn that a favourite fantasy was that of being a tyrannical king. Later, he commenced a strong friendship with his cousin, Roger de Bricqueville. The two were wont to indulge in a mutual "king and slave" fantasy. In this, and in other respects, they bore a close resemblance to the recent young Chicago murderers, Richard Loeb and Nathan Leopold, who also had a similar fantasy.* It is not impossible that some history of Gilles de Rais may have found its way into the hands of Leopold, who had a taste for the study of mediæval perversions.

Gilles' aptitude for soldiering must also be considered. It is probable that, by active service, he was able to divert part of his pathological tendencies into socially acceptable channels, to effect their "sublimation" as it is technically

* vide "The Case of Richard Loeb and Nathan Leopold," by M. Hamblin Smith and A. Fairweather, *Journal of Mental Science*, Jan., 1925.

called. War has had this effect upon many people. It would appear that society, periodically, finds that the restraints of modern civilisation are too severe ; all conventions are thrown aside, and the result is war. There were many manifestations during the late war which indicated the truth of this supposition. However this may be, Gilles exhibited courage and the capacity for leadership. This is what we should expect from a sadist. His supremacy fantasy was, no doubt, largely increased by his success in warfare.

Gilles was married at the age of sixteen. He had no affection for his wife, with whom he only cohabited for a few weeks, the result being the birth of a daughter, for whom also he showed little love. It is doubtful whether his guardian, who arranged the marriage, was aware of Gilles' homo-sexual tendencies. Probably he was not so aware. But if he was aware, and if he thought that he could counteract Gilles' homo-sexuality in this way, his efforts, as is always the case under these circumstances, were futile. Marriage always increases homo-sexuality. Some homo-sexuals have married, and have had children, in ignorance of their abnormal tendencies. This is a frequent cause of marital unhappiness. It is clear that women possessed no attraction for Gilles. His observed indifference to the lively ladies of the French Court, an indifference which was ascribed to a quite erroneous cause, is another indication of this. Joan of Arc appears to have had some influence over him. It is likely that Gilles' superstition, of which we shall speak directly, was stirred by Joan's claim to the possession of a divine mission.

After this episode, Gilles placed no bounds to his pathological traits. He lost pleasure in the vice he had hitherto practised. Sadistic cruelties took the vacant place. It is to be noted that these cruelties were always practised upon boys. That he was able to carry on his amazing murders for so long a time, was due partly to his exalted social position, and partly to the disturbed state of his country. His astonishing egotism is shown by his great prodigality, especially in the lavish production of theatrical performances. Then we must note his superstitious character, as indicated by his attempt to call in the assistance of demons, and his design of making atonement for his murders by the foundation and endowment of a religious institution. But it must not be supposed that Gilles was what is usually termed a hypocrite. It would appear that the remorse which he occasionally exhibited was quite genuine. There is also evidence that Gilles was unable to escape from his conscience, that is, as science would say, from the desire to live in accordance with what was approved by the general opinion of his time.

Gilles attributed a sex meaning to some of his alchemistic practices, a fact which is in accordance with the findings of psycho-analysis. That he took to drinking to excess is also in keeping with recent psycho-analytic theory, which is inclined to the view that all alcoholics are homosexual.

Readers will be certain to ask whether Gilles should be regarded as responsible for his actions. The answer will depend, to some extent, on whether legal or moral responsibility is meant. Let us consider the former question first. Very soon after Gilles' execution, an attempt was made to show that he had been mad. But this attempt emanated from his relations, whose object was to repudiate certain sales of land which he had made during the latter part of his life. The attempt failed. From the legal point of view, "insanity" is a purely social conception, and is not a medical conception. Society lays down certain rules of conduct, to which it requires its members to conform. Society reacts to those who commit breaches of these rules, the reaction usually taking the form of punishment. But when it can be shown that an offender suffers from one of certain mental abnormalities, the reaction of society is modified, the test being the presence of what is known as "insanity." The criterion of insanity is, speaking broadly, the nature of the ideas which govern, or appear to govern, the conduct of the offender. Certain ideas are regarded as delusions, that is to say, are regarded as being so absurd as to be evidence of insanity. Now, that Gilles, in legal phrase, knew the "nature and quality" of his acts there can be no doubt at all. And that he knew them to be wrong is shown by the fact that he took pains to destroy the evidence of his crimes. There is nothing in Gilles' murders which can be regarded as, in itself, proof of insanity. The murders can be paralleled in other cases, except as regards their great number. And there are even other mediæval instances of murder on a large scale. The only evidence of insanity in Gilles' case is his attempt to evoke demons.

How this practice would be taken depends upon the point of view of the age, showing how arbitrary is our conception of insanity. We may well compare the situation with that of spiritism. Let us ignore all the fraud which has played so large a part in this practice, and let us consider the case of an honest attempt to communicate with the spirits of the departed. Whether such communication is possible is beside the question. In the Middle Ages, communication with spirits, by the strict observance of certain rites, was regarded as quite possible, and was in no way looked upon as an insane delusion. The strict prohibition of the practice by ecclesiastical and civil law, and the severe penalties attached to it, are sufficient proof of this. A hundred years ago, the case would have been quite other. And it is likely that the practice of these mystic rites would, at that time, have been regarded as definite evidence of insanity. To-day, the case is changed again. Many people of education and intelligence hold, whether rightly or wrongly does not matter, that communication with spirits is possible. Such a belief would not now be taken as being, in itself, proof of insanity. Although, even now, the fact that a man asserted that he was in the habit of holding conversations with spirits would occasion grave suspicion as to his sanity, and would go far to excuse him from penal consequences of any criminal act which he might commit.

So we may take it that had Gilles committed some similar murders in this country, at the present day, he would be rightly regarded as being legally responsible for such actions. Modern psychologists are not disposed to admit the existence of what is usually termed "moral insanity," that is to say, insanity of conduct without intellectual disorder.

Was Gilles morally responsible? This question, like the former one, depends upon the point of view. Many are to-day inclined to take "morality" not in any absolute sense, but as a term for the general opinion of society in any given time and place. Modern scientific thought is tending ever more and more to the deterministic position, which holds that any given act was the only possible one which could have occurred under

Introduction

the particular circumstances. On this view, what was formerly known as "responsibility" does not exist in any case. Gilles' advocate, at the trial, took what practically amounted to this position, urging that Gilles was not responsible for his actions on account of demoniac possession. But the modern deterministic position in no way implies that people are to be allowed to do whatever they may please, without hindrance on the part of society. Society is bound to react, and always will react, against those who commit acts which tend to disturb its security. What this reaction may be is for society to determine, in each particular case. From his responsibility to this reaction, no man, sane or insane, can ever be free. A man "cannot help" being a man and not a horse. But he must accept the consequences of being a man and not a horse. One of these consequences is his liability to the reaction of society towards anti-social acts which he may commit.

The attitude of modern psychology towards crime is not one of blame, of judgment, or of criticism, but of unprejudiced investigation in a scientific spirit. It realises that neither society nor the offender understand the causes of their actions. Gilles certainly did not understand himself. He attempted some explanation of his conduct, but being quite ignorant of its causative factors, he was obliged to invent reasons, obliged to "rationalise." He attributed his conduct to his indulgent upbringing, an explanation which would be unthinkingly accepted by many people to-day, although it only contains a very small fraction of the truth. Modern psychology does not seek to control, but to guide the action of society, by supplying society with information about the offender, as also to assist the pathological personality by supplying it with information about itself. It holds that we cannot have too much light upon any case. It protests against the view that certain subjects are too objectionable for investigation. It holds that the more repulsive a subject is, the more it merits investigation, because it is certain to have become involved in a fog of prejudice. It welcomes books such as this. It finds in them not only an attempt to throw light upon dark cases of the past, but also an indication of the way in which puzzling cases of the present time should be approached.

M. HAMBLIN SMITH.

NOTE.—The authors accept no responsibility for the views expressed by Dr. Hamblin Smith.

CHAPTER I

EARLY YOUTH OF GILLES DE RAIS

FREUD asserts that every perverse tendency has its roots in childhood, and it is clear from the records of Gilles de Rais' life that the seeds of his degeneracy were sown in early youth.

The first glimpse we have of Gilles is at the age of fourteen, in the Castle of Champtocé on the borders of Brittany and Anjou. He is described, at this time, as being tall and graceful, with a lithe body, which concealed great physical strength, dark hair and eyes and an olive skin. Even at this age he was a precocious and vital personality. From the beginning there was something fatalistic in his life. Already he had been twice betrothed, first at the age of thirteen to Jeanne, daughter of Foulques Peynel, Lord of Hambuic and Briquebec, and a year later to

Beatrix, daughter of Alain IX, Viscount de Rohan and Count of Porhoet. The second nuptials had been made the occasion of a great gathering of the Breton nobility at the old capital of Vannes. By a strange and tragic coincidence both the brides selected for Gilles de Rais died.

Gilles' father had died when he was nine years old, and on the re-marriage of his mother, Gilles and his brother, René de la Suze, were entrusted to the care of their maternal grandfather, Jean de Craon. The younger brother, who resembled his mother's line, was Jean de Craon's favourite, and Gilles drifted into the habit of solitude which tended to darken and distort his outlook. His first years at Champtocé were taken up with field sports and study. He showed a phenomenal proficiency in everything he undertook, soon outdistancing his teachers and relying on his own capacity for acquiring knowledge.

Jean de Craon was too advanced in years to be equal to the task of disciplining Gilles, whose temperament made him unusually self-centred and intractable. He was the heir to vast wealth and great estates, and his knowledge of the fact was a strong incentive to his inherent egotism. In mind and body he was far in advance of his years. Instead of a gradual development of gifts or talents, Gilles possessed a mature and fully developed mind of unusual brilliancy. He was a genius who was too conscious of the fact. Perhaps because no one understood this complexity of character, self-admiration became a vice, and from the habit of basking in his own reflection the young Gilles developed a haughty pride and arrogance that would brook no restraint. He began early to exhibit a spirit of revolt and to impose his will on those around him.

Gilles' physical environment was not without

effect on his disposition. Raised on a rocky platform, overlooking the right bank of the Loire Champtocé was a forbidding structure of pillar and ramparts, drawbridge and moat, with subterranean galleries leading to the defence works. A turgid pond above the river level washed the gaunt granite sides of the towers. Although it was the smallest of Gilles' castles, a regal state, of which this lonely boy was the centre, was maintained. Cribbed and cabined, he lived in a world of one —himself, and introspection and morbidity became the forerunners of an interior life given over to unwholesome speculation. Since his mother's second marriage he had been entirely cut off from all womanly influence, and in this splendid isolation there was none near him sufficiently comprehending to gain his confidence or sympathy.

Allowing for these factors, all of which contributed to moulding his character at the plastic age, the taint in Gilles seems to have been self-germinated, fed on an exaggerated ego-consciousness. The virility of his adolescence craved action and impelled him with the desire to live the future in the instant. Hedged round with restrictions which limited the scope of his efforts, the life of the mind was the obvious way of escape, and he turned to his books. He read Valerius Maximus, Ovid's "Metamorphoses," the Annals of Tacitus and Saint Augustine's "City of God," and developed a remarkable proficiency in illuminating manuscripts and preparing decorative enamels. The habits of brooding and reflection which study engendered proved a pitfall.

It was a critical moment for Gilles when he took up the "Life of the Roman Emperors," a finely illustrated MS. of Suetonius. Their cruelties, their obscenities, and the despotic sway they wielded exercised a strong fascination for him. This was the man he would be, a king, a tyrant ruling by fear rather than by affection, bending everybody to his will. The rapture of the picture would leave him breathless, so that he would be compelled to fling the book aside and rush into the open to cool the fever which his emotions aroused. He went back again and again to the salacious history until it became an obsession. Many years after he admitted the deadly effect which this episode had upon him. "The said book was ornamented by pictures, very well printed, in which were seen the manner of life of the pagan emperors, and I read in the printed history how Caligula and other Cæsars sported with children and took singular pleasure in martyring them, upon which I desired to imitate the said Cæsars."

Gilles de Rais at sixteen formed a friendship with his cousin, Roger de Bricqueville, a youth of his own age, who had a disastrous influence over him. The two lads were the victims of a "king and slave" delusion. At first Gilles was the king and Roger the slave, but by degrees Bricqueville was able to reverse the order of the attraction by trading upon Gilles' susceptibility. He was the antithesis of Gilles in every way, and his apparent simplicity appealed to his cousin, whose superabundant intellectuality caused him to dislike anything approaching the same quality in his friends. Their companionship continued almost until the close of Gilles' life.

That Gilles' worst characteristics did not become evident much sooner than they did was due to a sudden upheaval which diverted the course of his early life.

CHAPTER II

WAR AND MARRIAGE

In the summer of 1420 news reached Champtocé that the Dauphin had imprisoned the Duke of Brittany in the Castle of Clisson and that civil war was imminent. Behind the century-old feud of the Montforts and Penthièvres, which divided Brittany in 1420, the Dauphin cloaked his private enmity against his brother-in-law, Duke Jean of Brittany. The Bretons had no love for the King of Bourges, as the Dauphin was contemptuously called, and the Duke had failed to carry out his promise to send troops against the English. By craftily using the quarrel of the Penthièvres for his own ends the Dauphin had succeeded in entrapping the Duke. The Duchess of Brittany, accompanied by her two children, appeared before the Breton *Etats Généraux*, convoked at Vannes on July 28, 1420, and made a passionate appeal for her husband.

Jean de Craon and Gilles, as Councillors of the Duchy, had been summoned to attend the parliament. It was Gilles' *début* in public life; and for the first time he came in touch with the world of men and affairs. The abruptness of the change from the imaginative life he had been leading to a life of action considerably modified his perspective. Whilst he had been wholly concerned with his lusts and his ambitions, his country was the centre of a heroic struggle. The English had mastered Normandy, and France was torn with the internal dissensions created by the rivalry of Jean Sans Peur of Burgundy and Bernard VII of Armagnac.

These reflections awakened no moral qualms in Gilles de Rais. Their effect was rather to stimulate his eagerness to achieve fame and power. It meant emerging into a wider horizon and realising some of his smouldering ambitions. His chivalry as well as his patriotism was stirred, and with his peers he swore on the cross to employ his body and his estates, and to give his whole heart even to the last drop of his blood to secure the deliverance of the Duke. Hitherto the houses of Laval and Craon had supported the Penthièvres, fighting alongside Charles de Blois, Guesclin and Clisson, but in common with all the Breton nobility they were now swept up in the call to their native loyalty. Fifty thousand Bretons, under Alain de Rohan, took the field.

Gilles raised several companies of men-at-arms, in addition to his grandfather's levies, and himself took command. One of the youngest captains serving, his daring, no less than his strategical ability, won him golden opinions. In view of the support in men and resources which Gilles' adherence to the Montfort cause represented, the Penthièvres concentrated their hostility against the Laval-Craon possessions. The barony of Rais and the Castle of La Motte-Achard in Poitou, along with many of Jean de Craon's estates, were ravaged. On their side the Montforts gave their opponents no rest, driving them from place to place until Jugon, Châteaulin, Brune and La Roche-Derrien fell. All the Breton efforts were then directed against Champtoceaux, where the Duke, after a series of adventures, had been finally imprisoned by Margaret de Clisson and her son Jean Sire de L'Aigle. On July 5 he capitulated and the Duke was released.

When the victorious Breton troops entered Nantes, Gilles rode with the Duke of Brittany and shared with his overlord the honours of the day. He found himself a hero, acclaimed on every side for his courage and resource. Duke Jean specially signalled him for honours and insisted upon making him a generous grant of fresh territorial possessions as a return for the aid given to his cause. Gilles found the glory of the occasion intoxicating. He declared that henceforward soldiering would be his profession, as it was that of his famous ancestors, Brumon de Laval and Bertrand du Guesclin. Jean de Craon thought the moment propitious to re-open the question of marriage, and was agreeably surprised to find a change in Gilles' attitude. His ward was enjoying his laurels, and nothing else mattered. The grandfather determined to profit by Gilles' tolerance, and without more preliminaries arranged a marriage between Gilles and Catherine, the sole heiress of Miles de Thouars.

Gilles was taken aback by this precipitancy and tried to defer a decision. There were considerations in favour of marriage. It would mean release from the nominal guardianship of his grandfather and control of his own wealth. The risk of being trammelled by a wife was of no great importance balanced against his ambitions, which, for the time being, swung higher than the temptation to revert to vice. However the tide went he would have no difficulty in subjugating his wife and, if necessary, disposing of her. Doubtless the novelty of the experience intrigued him. In the end he gave his consent, and Jean de Craon, overjoyed at the success of his move, hurried on the preparations for the marriage.

Having made his decision, Gilles entered into the spirit of the wedding festivities with zest. It meant another opportunity for attracting notoriety, and the adulation which he had already received for his share in the war had made him hungry for more. He became absorbed in the business of organising the celebrations, planning sumptuous entertainments for the guests, and composing special music for the Church service. The real object and significance of the occasion was completely forgotten in his interest in the arrangements, and the bride became merely a detail of the *mise-en-scène*, which was calculated to throw his own effulgence into greater relief.

In November 1420, the marriage, which was to prove a crucial test of Gilles' antipathy towards women, was celebrated. When the excitements of the event had cooled down Gilles was faced with an anti-climax in the shape of a sixteen-year-old wife for whom he had no affection. He was bored and irritated and took no pains to conceal his feelings. Catherine de Rais seems to have been a colourless sort of person and quite unfit to deal with the cryptic character of her husband. It was a union as incongruous as the mating of a lion and a lamb, and Gilles tired of married life almost before it had begun. After a brief honeymoon, he refused to cohabit with his wife. A girl child, Marie, was born to the youthful couple, but Gilles showed as little interest in her as in her mother. He was only happy amongst men and he realised, probably for the first time, that women were powerless to attract him. Catherine made several unsuccessful attempts to gain her boy husband's favour without in the least understanding the true cause of the estrangement. In Gilles' case normal sexual relationship had only resulted in confirming his unnatural repugnance towards women. An *impasse* had been reached, and, while Gilles was contemplating the best way to end it, the Penthièvres-Montfort quarrel threatened to break out afresh.

Gilles was again requested to attend a meeting of the States General, to debate the question of sending an embassy to England appealing for the release of the Comte de Richemont, who had been a prisoner there since Agincourt. Richemont was the one man able to handle the military situation, and Brittany and England were on friendly terms. He was overjoyed at the opportune excuse to leave his wife gracefully after twelve weeks of married misery, and Catherine, still unable to realise his intentions, retired to the Château of Pouzages in company with Jean de Craon. The second Penthièvres attempt was a comparatively tame affair. But it enabled Gilles to repeat his first success, and brought him prominently under the notice of that great soldier, Richemont, who had marked him out as a man who would go far.

CHAPTER III

THE EAGLET

DURING the year in which Gilles had been absent, the administration of his estates had been handed over to Roger de Bricqueville, against the advice of Jean de Craon. It was obviously impossible for a mere youth to control so large a heritage, and the chaos which resulted from the attempt was the initial step in Gilles' financial misfortune. Bricqueville was thoroughly unprincipled and, like all Gilles' intimates, feathered his own nest at the expense of the wayward millionaire.

Gilles' possessions had been enormously increased by his marriage, and it would be impossible to estimate accurately the extent of his wealth. From his father, Guy de Laval, Lord of Clisson, he had inherited the castle and estates of Machecoul,

St. Etienne de la Mer Morte, Pornic, Princay and Vue, as well as the island of Bouin with its fortress. On the maternal side he held the Hôtel de la Suze at Nantes, famous for its priceless Flemish and Italian tapestries, the castle and lands of Briolley, Champtocé, Ingrandes, in Anjou; Sénéché, Grattecuisse, Lorous, Bottereau, La Benasté and Bourgneuf-en-Rais. His wife brought him as her wedding portion the great estate of Tiffauges, Pouzages, Chabannis, Confolens, Châteaumorant, Savenay and Lombert. And this represented only his principal properties. Gilles inherited, as well, a colossal fortune in gems, tapestries and gold and silver *objets de vertu*. As Lord of the Barony of Rais, bounded on the north by the Loire, on the west by the Atlantic, eastwards by the further shore of the Lac de Grandlieu, and on the south by the frontiers of Poitou, Gilles de Rais at the age of eighteen was

The Château of Tiffauges at the present day.

the doyen of all the *seigneurs* in Brittany. It would have been strange if, with all his millions and a wife he did not want, he had kept his head.

After twelve months of hard fighting he was in a mood for any wildness. He had had no opportunity of enjoying his heritage and was intent on making the most of it. Freed from all restraints, and with his wife away at Pouzages, Gilles proceeded to enjoy his licence to the full. It commenced with a series of state visits to his castles, and at each halt there were feastings and receptions on a prodigious scale.

On the occasion of his marriage he had produced at Angers a morality play, consisting of a series of *tableaux vivants* copied from the tapestries in the choir of the Cathedral of Notre Dame. Several companies of players were now brought specially from Paris to follow in his train. The *Clercs de la Basoche* appeared at all the receptions in short morality plays, which were the most popular form of drama, and the *jongleurs* and *enfants sans souci* performed witty and often mordant satires. Gilles wrote many of the satires himself and frequently played in them.

His flamboyant egotism was gratified by the stir which his presence everywhere aroused, and the sumptuousness of the entertainments he gave had become the talk of France. The King of Anjou and the Duke of Brittany tried to follow his lead, but they had neither the wealth nor the artistry. Gilles' most striking triumph was at Champtocé, whither the Dauphin had come as the guest of honour. In all France there was no such magnificence as in the castle on the banks of the Loire. The walls were covered with cloth of gold, the floors tiled with white marble and jade, and the ceilings decorated by the greatest Italian artists. Every bed-chamber had its ewers of gold, embossed after Grecian designs, and filled with mélisse and rose water. From the old records we learn something of the dishes offered to the Dauphin. There were pasties of beef, pies of leveret and small birds heavily spiced, heron, swan, crane, buzzard, roast stork, lampreys, and salads of briony and mallow sprinkled with mace, carraway, poppy, rosemary, hyssop and ginger. The drinks were dry wines, and hypocras, beer and fermented mulberry juice. Musicians played before and during the banquets, and as a prelude to the theatricals an Arab dancer performed the Moresque.

Gilles was in his element at these spectacular functions. An eye-witness of the time describes him as "a real hero of majestic appearance, seductive face, graceful, petulant, with a lively and playful spirit, but weak and frivolous."

If Gilles enjoyed all this splendour, poor Catherine

de Rais and Jean de Craon were at their wits' ends. They had been brought from their seclusion for the sake of appearance to meet the Dauphin, but it was clear, at least to Jean de Craon, that the marriage was foredoomed. Strictly speaking, Jean de Craon's guardianship extended until Gilles was eighteen, but as an inducement to obtaining his grandson's assent to the marriage he had agreed to relinquish his stewardship. He now bitterly regretted his action. Not only was the alliance, on which he had placed all his hopes, a failure, but Gilles' folly and prodigality was another source of anxiety. It was what he had feared might happen. Gilles' sudden accession to wealth had completely upset his balance. To the flood of sycophants who surrounded him he dispensed money and gifts without stint or excuse. Even the Dauphin borrowed freely to replenish the royal exchequer.

Jean de Craon was less concerned about the squandering of money than the condition of mind which it indicated. He knew that the life Gilles was leading must be morally disintegrating, and that it was only a matter of time until he returned to his former habits. And it was the truth. Gilles had reached a stage when his inchoate feelings demanded something more than luxury and aesthetic display. It was the beginning of another protracted spell of viciousness in which everything else was forgotten. Most of his associates were men of his own station, but indulgence soon weakened his pride of rank. Pages, men-at-arms, and servants, if they attracted the attention of their noble master, were made the recipients of his bounty. A young man named Henri Griart, who acted as librarian, became the boon companion of Gilles, who professed a great admiration for his erudition. Bricqueville aided and abetted Gilles in his orgies, knowing this to be the surest way of consolidating his position.

Gilles' spells of debauchery were followed by fits of melancholy. The realisation of his gifts, the knowledge that he was wasting his time and energy upon profligate living, and that he was fast becoming a slave to vice, were all set against the vision of himself as the man he might be. In these moods he would fly into violent rages and no one would venture near him while they lasted. His ego had a Jekyll and Hyde capacity, now urging him to depravity and then propelling him to self-fulfilment by the utilisation of his undoubted gifts. Ideas were as dangerous to him as explosives in the hands of a child, and the passive life meant a mind constantly turning over the possibilities of new sins, the exploring of fresh obscenities. With action, his morbidity dispersed, and he lived to astonish the world by performing prodigies of valour and unexpected acts that revealed his penetrating intellect and rare faculty of initiative.

Fortunately for Gilles, the political situation continued to develop on lines favourable to his career, and for this consummation Jean de Craon was mainly responsible. On the inspiration of Yolande of Aragon, mother of the Dauphin, he rallied Brittany to the French cause. When the Dauphin arrived at Saumur to meet the Duke of Brittany on September 8, 1422, and settle the terms of a proposed alliance with France, Jean de Craon utilised the occasion for bringing the Dauphin on a visit to Champtocé. His object in arranging this meeting between the future Charles VII and his grandson was that Gilles might be tempted to abandon his vicious life, and take his proper place in the councils of the nation. His move was entirely successful. The moment was propitious. Gilles was sick of himself and his friends, and it pleased him to be mixing again with men of his own social and intellectual calibre. His flamboyant personality and wit completely captivated the Dauphin, who was as much impressed by the grandeur of Champtocé as he was by its youthful lord. Compared to it, his own Court was but a poor place. He was only twenty-two, and he envied Gilles his wealth and freedom from responsibility.

When the Dauphin returned to Paris, Gilles accompanied him. For nearly a year Gilles remained at Court, taking advantage of every opening to impress himself on the Dauphin and his circle. Georges la Tremoille, the power behind the weak-willed ruler of France, was specially impressed by Gilles, and attributed his indifference to the gallantries and amenities of the Court to the young seigneur's high and serious purpose.

This was, of course, an over-generous estimate. Gilles had no interest in the frail and fair ladies who sought his favour and his riches, and, for the time, ambition swamped everything else. He was satisfied when the Dauphin, at the suggestion of Richemont, offered him the important military command of the border country between Maine and Anjou. The Anglo-Burgundians were harrying all this country.

Gilles returned at once to Champtocé, and raised fresh companies amongst his own adherents. When he took the field he speedily proved his mettle, fighting with such famous soldiers as La Hire and the Marshals Bussac and La Fayette. With the Sieurs of Beaumanoir and Loré singly and with combined forces, Gilles became the dread of the English. At Montargis Gilles fought with a dash that amazed everyone. Again at Ambières, where the French troops were greatly outnumbered, Gilles won fresh laurels. He was the first to take the fortress of Lude, and engaged Blackburn, the English commander, in hand-to-hand combat. Blackburn, who had sworn to resist to the death, went down with Gilles' sword in his throat.

War does not turn men into angels, and we know that the effect of an orgy of killing upon those who are psychically unstable may be brutalising. As his after-life proved, Gilles had all the instincts of the sadist, to whom cruelty is a necessary part of sexual gratification. From his first break into abnormality he had, on his own confession, desired to kill and mutilate. That this savage lust to take life was suppressed for some years might reasonably be put down to the licence afforded to shed blood by methods which civilisation has ever regarded as legitimate and praiseworthy. There is no need to emphasize the abyss separating warfare from acts of obscene cruelty, but as a means of diagnosing Gilles de Rais the psychological reactions to warfare cannot be ignored. Gilles was noted for his ferocity on the battle-field, and there is little doubt that this was the outcome of his submerged cruelty and viciousness. There was an instance of this at Rainefort, where amongst the garrison of the captured city were some French mercenaries. The other commanders were for pardoning them, but Gilles insisted they should be summarily hanged, and stood by while his orders were carried out.

It is difficult to establish whether Gilles indulged in vice during his campaign or not. Arthur de Richemont would certainly have shown little consideration to young officers, no matter how distinguished, of proclivities such as Gilles had displayed in the past. That he gained Richemont's respect is a point in his favour.

Gilles' sins were not broadcasted to the world, and only during his trial was the full story made known. Even then, however, nothing was said about his life while he bore arms, and he himself was silent on this point. Some redeeming spark of decency, no doubt, urged him to dissociate the best part of his life from the foulness of the aftermath.

CHAPTER IV

GILLES AND SAINT JOAN

It was at Chinon, on February 23, 1429, towards evening, that Gilles de Rais met Joan of Arc for the first time. She had arrived to interview the Dauphin, accompanied by Jean de Metz and Bertrand de Poulengy. Around the Dauphin, in the immense hall of the Castle crowded with three hundred lords and knights, stood Regnault de Chartres, Chancellor of France and Archbishop of Rheims; Tremoille the Court Chancellor, Raoul de Gaucourt, Grand Master of the King's Household, and Gilles de Rais. The atmosphere was one of incredulity that the Dauphin should deign to receive this eighteen-year-old peasant girl, and hostility to her fantastic claims and pretensions. From the moment of the Maid's appearance, Gilles stood out as her friend and champion. Against the scepticism of the Dauphin and the Court, he insisted in his belief in her divine mission to save France. His cousins, Guy and André de Laval, the Count d'Alençon and Dunois, the Bastard of Orleans, followed his lead.

The impression made by Joan on such a man as Gilles de Rais is a mystery. It might be argued that his impressionable and volatile temperament caught quickly any contagion of enthusiasm or novelty, or that his superstitious nature (and he was superstitious) was affected by Joan's talk of Voices and other mystical manifestations. A far more likely view is that his religious sense, always dormant, was quickened by Joan's sanctity. When the Dauphin finally entrusted the command of the armies to the Maid, Gilles, at her own request, was made her protector on the field.

The Maid herself was full of gratitude for

Gilles' friendship. Perhaps her discerning eye saw some predestination in the attachment, and, certainly, her native shrewdness recognised how much was to be gained by having her decisions and authority supported by one who stood so high at Court. Often it was their joint will that broke down the opposition of rival commanders, jealous of their reputations. There was one instance in particular when Regnault de Chartres, the chief agent of Tremoille, strove to oppose Joan's design, and Gilles, resisting all rebuffs, violently combated Chartres' plan, which on the face of it seemed the only one. It was a big risk which might have decided the fate of Orleans, and as usually happened Joan was right.

The army set out for the great adventure on April 27, 1429, Joan at the head, riding between Gilles de Rais and her squire, Jean d'Aubon. During the action against the Forts of St. Augustine and St. Jean le Blanc, Joan was wounded, and in the panic which followed she was deserted by all but Gilles. The Maid never forgot his devotion and bravery, and it was on this occasion she referred to Gilles as her "faithful and valorous companion." When Joan had made up her mind to return to Blois to provide herself with a supporting force for her attack on the Tourelles, Dunois begged Gilles to use his influence to prevent Joan from leaving them at such a critical time. Upon Gilles promising to make the journey in her stead, she agreed to remain. After the victory of Orleans the success of the campaign was greatly hindered by lack of the resources of war. Joan could hope for no material assistance from the Dauphin, and again Gilles stepped into the breach. With his cousins the Lavals, he mortgaged some of his estates to increase the personnel for the attack on Jargeau, where Suffolk and other English nobles were captured.

Gilles' co-operation with Joan throughout the hostilities set the seal upon his career, and greatly strengthened his power. He was able to counter Tremoille's manœuvre against Richemont, who was in temporary disgrace. The Dauphin accepted Gilles' bond guaranteeing Richemont's fidelity, and the Constable was restored to the position from which the favourite had ousted him. In July, the Dauphin was crowned at Rheims, and Gilles was made a Marshal of France. He was one of the four Knights chosen to head the imposing cavalcade which brought the Holy Oil from the Abbey of Saint Rémy to Rheims. The ceremony has been described in a letter sent by Pierre de Beauvais to the King of Sicily, from which the following extract is taken :

"First of all clad in armour and with their

banner displayed, the Lord de Rais, the Marshals de Boussac and Graville and the Admiral de Coulant and a great company rode out to meet the Abbot and bring back the Holy Oil. They rode into the minster at Rheims, and alighted at the entrance to the Choir. The Archbishop administered the coronation oath, he crowned and anointed the King, while all the people cried ' Noel,' and the trumpets sounded so that you might think the roof might be rent."

Two months later, the King by royal letters patent authorised " Gilles de Rais and Pouzages, Marshal of France, in recognition of his glorious service and to perpetuate their memory, to show in his coat of arms a bordering of fleur de lys." A similar honour was conferred upon Joan and her descendants. Gilles was only twenty-five years of age when he thus attained the summit of his ambitions, and it is a striking commentary

GILLES DE RAIS
From a portrait by Montfaucon.

upon the manner in which they had been realised that he reached fulfilment through humility and the surrender of his will to a higher purpose.

Immediately after the coronation, resisting the King's invitation to remain at Court, Gilles rejoined the army of the Maid at Senlis. Their forces marched on Paris with the Duke d'Alençon and Louis d'Anjou in the centre, and Gilles and the Marshal de Bussac in command of the two wings. On September 8th, the royal army divided into two sections and commenced the attack on Paris. The first army was under the command of Joan, with Gilles and Goncourt as her lieutenants. Gilles led the attack on the Gates of St. Honoré, while the Duke d'Alençon covered his advance. During the progress of fight, the King had received an envoy from the Duke of Burgundy begging him to cease hostilities and promising to yield up Paris. The easily-fooled Dauphin sent orders to his commanders to cease action, but Joan, ignoring the royal orders, continued the struggle. She was wounded in the thigh, and Gilles remained beside her all day. It was their last rally together. For some unknown reason the King, whose heart had never been in the fight, peremptorily ordered Gilles to rejoin him. And so it was that at the hour of Joan's capture Gilles was not there.

Between September, 1429, and November, 1430, there is no trace of Gilles' movements. The probability is that he was furious at the King's ingratitude and duplicity and had retired to one of his castles. One cannot imagine the tempestuous nature of Gilles submitting tamely to the injustice perpetrated against the Maid. In November he re-appeared suddenly in the vicinity of Louviers, some sixteen miles from Rouen, with two armed companies. He had evidently some idea of using Louviers as a base against the English in combination with La Hire and the Duke d'Alençon. Underneath the daring adventure of retaking Rouen there was the plan of rescuing Joan from her captors. Gilles would have had little difficulty in gaining the consent of that dashing cavalry leader La Hire to such an enterprise, and *le Beau Duc*, who had always been one of the Maid's staunchest champions, would have needed no coaxing. The English command got wind of the plot, and threatened to throw the Maid into the Seine rather than relinquish their prize. For six months the three courageous chevaliers vainly dashed their forces against the English stronghold in the hope of saving Joan.

On June 1st, news arrived of Joan's martyrdom. It is impossible to over-estimate the crushing and destructive effect of the blow on Gilles de Rais. To see the Saint defamed and done to death as a "sorceress, a divineress, a false prophet, one who worked with evil spirits, a witch, a heretic, an apostate, a seditious blasphemer, rejoicing in bloodshed, and indecent," was unsupportable. Heaven seemed to have turned a deaf ear to one of her own; the world was no longer sane, when purity and truth were defeated and evil triumphed. We can imagine with what saturnine gibe of defiance, almost in the spirit of a monstrous jest, he swore that henceforth he would serve evil alone. As he had been linked with Joan in all that had been glorious and noble, so would he take upon himself actually to commit those crimes laid to her account which he knew existed only in the imagination of her judges. He would blaspheme, evoke evil spirits, deal in sorcery, rejoice in bloodshed and indecency. He may well have fallen into a state of mind akin to madness.

Even yet, Gilles was hardly able to convince himself that his innocent girl comrade was dead. When the false Pucelle, Jeanne d'Armentières, appeared, Gilles, for a time, believed that the Maid had escaped death by a miracle. For some months he employed himself in fugitive fighting exploits in the attempt to shake off the creeping moral paralysis that had overtaken him, and his intense hatred for the English found vent in a wild and futile plot to kidnap the young English King, Henry VI, at Rouen. Disillusioned, he returned to Champtocé, ensnared by his old personality. Warfare, honour, and ambition had lost their appeal and life its savour.

If we would realise fully the change in Gilles' outlook after Joan's death, it is necessary to grasp the extraordinary revolution in his character which association with the Maid had brought about. It would have been easier for Gilles to overcome his vice than his pride. The constant presence of the Maid, and the atmosphere of spirituality which was always with her, was an incentive to decent living which even Gilles de Rais could not resist.

To replace humility by egotism was a more difficult task. Gilles de Rais surrendered all. It was a new and ennobled Gilles who rode by the Maid's side and shared her fortunes. In the manner of his acceptance of her end we see something more than the fatal reversion to the old instincts and sway. He was at the pinnacle of his fame, still a very young man, with a quality of resource capable of carrying him to any length. But his ambition was offered as a sacrifice in the flames that destroyed the Maid. It was a gesture worthy of this strange character, an extremist in everything and not without a certain nobility hidden in the undergrowth of his vices. His new-born idealism had perished and the satyr and murderer lay in waiting to fill the gap.

We may regret that Joan's ennobling influence had no permanence, but that it was even allowed to fall upon such barren soil must be wonder enough. In his end, too, there was an echo of Joan's spirit. Modern psychologists, with some notable exceptions, will have nothing to do with the phenomena of sanctity and seek a physical explanation for everything in the universe. With this limitation we have no sympathy. We accept the influence of Joan of Arc upon Gilles de Rais as possessing a distinct supernatural value, incapable of rationalistic solution.

When we remember Gilles' fanatical dislike of women, his epicureanism and egotism, and above all, the evil depth of his nature, and find that his whole soul, happiness and fame were pivoted on the Maid, no other inference is possible.

The sensualist and potential murderer, the ego-maniac, whose falcon-like spirit derided all other dominance, was completely subjugated by the simplicity of the saintly peasant girl. For the fatality which dogged the rest of Gilles' life we must blame his own moral weakness, and, in a contributory degree, Joan's executioners. The problem of evil is not to be explained away by any psychological ingenuities. It will always remain an individual problem, to be fought by weapons not found in any laboratory or scientific textbook.

CHAPTER V

AESTHETE AND MURDERER

GILLES de Rais arrived at Champtocé in December, 1432, recalled by the death of Jean de Craon. Bricqueville still occupied the post of major-domo, but Gilles had discovered a new favourite, Gilles de Sillé, who accompanied him to Champtocé.

They had met at Lagny in August, and Gilles, recognising in Sillé the traits which he looked for in his familiars, induced him to leave the army. This friendship marked the parting of the ways. When Gilles permanently abandoned his career his normal life ceased to function. He was a man thrown back upon himself and cut adrift from his moorings. The old egomania was again dominant and there was nothing to hinder its action. To his uncontrolled lust there was now added a definite purpose. From Gilles himself we learn that his days and nights, during this period, were spent " drinking and rejoicing with Gilles de Sillé." It almost seemed that he was trying to drug whatever remnant of conscience remained.

In the church of St. Hilaire de Poitiers, of which Gilles by virtue of his fiefs was a lay canon, there was a boy from La Rochelle whose wonderful singing had earned for him the name of the Rossignol. This youth was to prove the first link in the chain of circumstances which opened the era of horror in the life of Gilles de Rais. The Rossignol's physical perfection matched his voice. He was a Greek type and blonde, with a finely shaped head covered with close curling hair. All Gilles' perverted love of beauty was awakened by the Rossignol. To tempt the boy, Gilles settled upon him the princely gift of the Rivière estate, close to Machecoul, which brought in a substantial revenue, and gave his parents three hundred crowns. Nobody suspected Gilles' real motive in going to such extravagant lengths, with the exception of a corrupt cleric, called Eustace Blanchet. His reckless expenditure in everything pertaining to his Church services was notorious. For three copes he had on one occasion paid fourteen thousand golden crowns. His ecclesiastical household numbered over eighty persons and included the clergy of a cathedral church, an archdeacon, a dean, a vicar, canons, chaplains, co-adjutors, cantors, a schoolmaster, clerks, and numberless choristers. The chief dignitary had been styled "Bishop" by Gilles, but the title was quite unauthorised. In all this external display there was not a grain of genuine devotion, nothing save aestheticism run mad, a destructive pride akin to that of Lucifer.

In addition to the gifts made to the Rossignol, and the flatteries showered upon him, he was promised a post of great trust when he reached manhood. The report of Gilles' generosity to the choir-boy spread far and wide, drawing many other youths, who came from long distances, hoping to find a place in the Lord de Rais' choir. In their train followed young beggars. The Rossignol had all unconsciously proved a decoy for others, and the import of this was not lost on Gilles. All the principal members of his household were despatched to his various castles, and upon Roger de Bricqueville devolved the task of interviewing and selecting the prospective victims.

Gilles had become more and more brutalised. Encouraged by the presence and active participation of his two accomplices, his sadistic tendencies were now getting the upper hand. In Gilles de Rais' nature there existed a sense of brutality, as real as that of hunger or thirst, which periodically demanded satisfaction, and now his satiated lusts were driving him to more intensive forms of brutality. His sadism was not likely to restrict itself to those acts of violence, such as flagellation, which content the ordinary sadist, and could only be satisfied by the infliction of intense suffering and the spilling of blood. There had come back to his mind, if ever it was really absent, the phrase from Suetonius of how the Caesars "sported with children and took singular pleasure in martyring them." The idea enslaved him, and he seriously considered making his first experiment with the Rossignol, but the choirboy's voice fascinated him and he decided to look elsewhere for a victim. Neither Bricqueville nor Sillé guessed what was passing in Gilles' mind, but even had they known, their own sordid depravity was equal to that of Gilles.

Although the names of many of those whom Gilles de Rais murdered were made known during his trial, there is no record as to the identity of his first victim. In his savage blood-hunger he determined that the youth to be immolated should be strong and vigorous, so that there should be enough resistance to whet his desire, but he had underestimated his power of control. Unnatural excitement had produced a temporary cessation of the moral and mental faculties, and brutal horseplay succeeded the usual orgies. Gilles dealt the first blow and Sillé hardly conscious of impending tragedy, followed his example. Flogging and beating by two drunken perverts, who tried to outdo each other, culminated in Gilles stabbing, and afterwards strangling, his victim.

A suite of apartments formerly used as a *salle d'armes*, and situated in a remote part of the Château, was set apart for the "sport of the Caesars." One room was occupied by Gilles as a bedroom, and the apartment adjoining was used as the abattoir. He had tasted blood and had found, as he afterwards admitted, that murder, for its own sake, gave him more relish than lust. The bodies of the victims were thrown into a dry well, where they were safe from observation, and it sometimes happened that Gilles fell asleep in the room where the murder had been done, with the broken and defiled human remains within sight of where he lay.

In all, forty youths were done to death before Gilles de Rais' mania was appeased. It may seem incredible that it was possible for him to exterminate so many boys without any news of his crimes reaching the outside world. The reason was that his position as a feudal chief, almost akin to a petty monarch, made his acts practically immune from question. No one would have dared to connect him with the disappearance of the boys, the majority of them parentless, who entered Champtocé—never again to leave its grim portals. Added to this, the condition of the country, torn by the Hundred Years' War, made concern or discovery highly improbable. The widespread poverty and constant alarms had scattered thousands of the population far from their hearths. For a child to vanish in a land infested by the enemy, English and Burgundian, as well as by French brigands, would excite neither interest nor surprise. Even the thieves were alarmed at the appearance of the lean gaunt labourers who roamed from place to place seeking food.

After the fortieth murder Gilles moved to Machecoul. There was no pause in the sanguinary acts with which he had befouled Champtocé. Sillé used a diabolic ingenuity in devising new methods of sadistic outrage, after the example of Charles, King of Navarre.* Only by such means could he hope to retain the favour of his master. At times he quailed before his ferocity, filled with apprehension that his own life might be forfeited in one of Gilles' frenzies. More than once he thought of cutting loose, but fear of the consequences, and financial considerations, overcame his scruples. At Machecoul, the same number of murders were committed as at Champtocé. For some unaccountable reason, there was always an interval after the fortieth murder; this, apparently, was the number of victims necessary for the gorging of the monster's blood lust.

We come now to an episode which might be

* Burned alive for his heinous crimes in 1387.

taken to indicate that conscience was stirring in the mass-murderer. The truth is, however, that Gilles' only show of real contrition was at the end, and this act, with its suggestion of remorse, merely adds to the bewildering contradictions of his character. It is one of the characteristic phenomena of his life that he seems to have been, until the end, quite unable to recognise the enormity of his guilt. In almost every case of an individual habituated to any form of aberration the amount of regret is usually in an inverse ratio to the frequency of the lapses. The first crime, whether it be petty theft or murder, is, according to the degree of normal consciousness, the most atrocious and the most far-reaching in its after-effects. Where the moral and social sense is lacking, as it was with Gilles de Rais, satisfaction may take the place of contrition. Every true criminal is an anarchist, and therefore an ego-maniac, who rejoices in his capacity to break laws and hurt his fellows. As we have seen, egotism was the chief source of Gilles' criminality, and it was this self-glorification which prevented him from ever seeing himself and his acts in their right perspective.

Now, after a year of vice and bloodshed, his twisted mind formulated the idea of commemorating his victims in some pious manner. The more thought he gave to the idea the more his complacency increased. There was a deep and unconscious irony in the plan, which was that of a Foundation dedicated to the Holy Innocents to be erected at Machecoul. The man who had out-Heroded Herod could thus insure his soul against the damnation he had so richly earned, and at the same time raise a memorial to his own piety. Such an astounding paradox simply baffles analysis. It is too colossal to be dismissed by a term so weak as hypocrisy, too grotesque to be measured by any known gauge of conduct. It was megalomania *in excelsis*.

The document giving details of the Foundation,* which was drafted later by Jean Casan and Jean de Recouin, two notaries of Orleans, conveyed to the King and Duke all the revenues that Gilles had ever inherited or might in the future inherit from his ancestors to the fourth degree, always with the proviso that the princes were to maintain the Foundation in memory of the Holy Innocents. And if they refused the bequests on those terms, the upkeep of the Chantry was entrusted, on the same conditions, to the King of France, and if the King of France refused, the Emperor (Louis of Bavaria) was specified. Failing the Emperor, the Pope (Eugenius IV) was asked to accept the trust. Finally, if the

* vide Appendix III.

Pope refused, the Knights of St. John of Jerusalem and of St. Lazarus were designated, each Order to hold half the endowments. To ensure his wishes being carried out, Gilles expressed the hope that the ecclesiastical authority would, under the penalty of excommunication, compel his heirs to carry out his wishes in the matter.

SIGNATURE OF GILLES DE RAIS

The erstwhile choir-boy, Rossignol, was made treasurer of the Chapter, and the members of his clergy appointed to the various offices. For the time murder had ceased, and the organisation of the Chantry occupied all Gilles' attention. He was again the alert and vital personality, his mind untroubled by any shadow of his manifold crimes. His boundless vitality made movement essential, and the direction of his energies was always determined by his abnormality. After the riot of murder he felt the need for relaxation. His theatrical sense longed again for the limelight, bade him strut and posture and artificially revive the glories of his heroic days. This was to be the next phase.

CHAPTER VI

ACTOR—MANAGER—PRODUCER

THE recrudescence of Gilles de Rais' stage mania, which had first shown itself in his boyhood, was, as we have already hinted, closely allied to his sexual abnormality and a component element of the whole morbid diathesis. It was not the result of any genuine histrionic ability or legitimate love of the drama, but a symptom consistent with his diseased egotism and perverted instincts. René de la Suze declared that the theatre was one of the principal causes of his brother's ruin, a statement that is amply confirmed by the facts.

To the playgoing public who are accustomed to the wonderful productions of the modern theatre it will come as a surprise to learn that Gilles de Rais was a forerunner of this movement. Indeed it is debatable whether the stage of to-day could give us anything approaching in cost or display the "shows" mounted by Gilles in the years 1433-1434.

Murderer, millionaire, actor, soldier, disciple of aesthetics and satyr—it is a bizarre combination, but all these elements were cogs in the wheel of Gilles de Rais' mental machinery. Play-acting was no novelty to him and his patronage of the mediaeval drama was of no distant date, but his latest departure dwarfed all previous efforts. A company of actors was attached to his household in the same manner as his clergy and military staff. The services of poets and writers were engaged to compose plays after Gilles' ideas, and costumes, decorations and properties were manufactured under his personal supervision. There is no doubt that Gilles started a fashion which became popular in his own time and continued to develop after his death.

We find one of his cousins producing "*Sainte Barbe*" at Laval, and René of Anjou almost beggared himself in trying to outdo Gilles. Incidentally Gilles himself was made bankrupt by this passion for the stage. His programme, which was at first designed for his own and his retainers' amusement, consisted of farces, pantomimes and *soties*—the latter a mixture of the morality play and the farce. As the magnitude of his productions increased, his enthusiasm grew, and the public were admitted without payment to all the performances. Those in humble stations were fitted with costly robes, in order that their appearance should harmonize with the *ensemble*, and strike no jarring note. Ten productions were staged, mainly at Champtocé, the cost of one alone being fifty thousand golden crowns.

Feeling that his genius was being circumscribed, and that the reverberations of his greatness and versatility did not do justice to his efforts, Gilles arranged to make a triumphal tour of the principal towns in Brittany. Everybody of note from the King downward should be invited to the performances, so that the occasion might be stamped upon the imagination of the world at large. He travelled in regal state, and his entry into, and exit from, the various centres were marked with a ceremony more usually associated with the movement of the Court.

Gilles and his company visited, amongst other places, Nantes, Bourges, Angers, and Montluçon. Christmas, Easter and Whitsun were the times chosen for his theatrical seasons.

The transport of players, musicians, and stage properties was responsible for an enormous amount of trouble and expense, but this was nothing compared to the advertisement which it brought to the star performer. At Nantes a herald, accompanied by four men-at-arms, made the following announcement: " We, Noble and Powerful Baron, Gilles de Rais, Marshal of France, Lord of Champtocé, Tiffauges, Machecoul, St. Etienne de la Mer Morte, Pornic and other places, do by these presents make known that by permission of the High and Powerful Lord Seigneur, Jean de Malestroit, by the Grace of God and the Holy Father, Bishop of Nantes, there will be given on the twenty-first day of the present month, two o'clock afternoon, at the Place of Notre Dame, a representation of a Mystery concerning the Life of Our Lord and of Madame the Holy Virgin His Mother." The crowd responded with cries of " Liesse, Liesse to the Marshal, Liesse to the Lord Bishop."

On the day of the performance the Lord de

Rais and his suite left the Hôtel de la Suze with a guard of honour in casque and cuirass, Damascene steel halberds and scabbards glittering in the sun. The soldiers with their halberds pressed back the gaping crowd from too close proximity to the most powerful noble in Brittany. By Gilles' side walked an aide-de-camp holding an upturned casque filled with coined money, which Gilles scattered right and left. So great was the interest created by Gilles' grand tour that practically all industry was stopped during the performances, and people were obliged under the penalty of a heavy fine to attend. This compulsory support of the drama lends quite a Shavian touch to the proceedings and is a measure which would commend itself to the touring actor of to-day.

The climax of Gilles' theatrical venture was a production of the " *Mystère du Siège d'Orléans*," which was given at the town so closely connected with the memory of Joan. News of the spectacle and the unprecedented preparation which Gilles had made attracted wide-spread attention, and Charles VII intimated his intention of being present at the opening. In September, 1434, Gilles de Rais and a retinue of nearly one thousand persons arrived at Orleans. There was a personal guard of two hundred knights, squires and pages, splendidly equipped, with his clergy, college house, musicians, and choristers, in addition to five hundred actors. Gilles' brother, René de la Suze, accompanied him on this occasion—the only time on record in their later life when they were together. His presence was due to the suggestion of the family, who hoped that he might restrain Gilles' insensate waste of money.

Gilles' one idea was to make himself the observed of all observers and to blaze a trail which no one could hope to follow. Every available hostelry in Orleans and the surrounding district was taxed to its capacity to provide accommodation for Gilles and his army of retainers. The town was *en fête*, and the approach of the gorgeously mounted host was such a sight as the inhabitants of Orleans had never seen since the day when Joan's victorious army entered the town. An enormous stage that could support the moving crowds taking part in the battle scenes was erected, and in a cave under the stage were stored barrels of hypocras and fine vintages for the refreshment of performers and spectators. Gilles, with mad extravagance, insisted that fresh costumes should be worn at every performance and the old ones discarded.

It was said in Orleans that " none remembered, or ever expected to see such superfluity, excess and unreasonable expenditure," but the thing which intrigued everybody was that the real Gilles de Rais was billed to play the stage Gilles de Rais. Another interesting amateur actor was Prégent de Coëtivy, Chamberlain to Charles VII, Admiral of France and Governor of La Rochelle, who afterwards became Gilles' son-in-law.

Charles VII was included amongst the *dramatis personae*, and this fact increased the desire of the King to see himself as others saw him. From a dramatic point of view it was a startling innovation on Gilles' part to present the stage embodiments of living personages to themselves. The "*Mystère du Siège d'Orléans*" is a curiosity of dramatic literature. The MS. of the play is now in the Vatican Library, but there is a version extant compiled by Guessard and Certain from the original which appears in the "*Collection des Documents inédits de l'Histoire de France.*" It contains one hundred and forty distinct *rôles* and 20,529 lines. The scenes include the vision of Joan whilst tending her sheep and her first interview with the King. Another is laid in England, showing the enemy preparations for the expedition against France, followed by scenes of the relief of Orleans and the return to the city after the victory of Patay. The verses display neither literary quality nor dramatic interest, defects which were of minor importance in a spectacle so gigantic. What really mattered were the *tableaux* and battle scenes, the mounting, dressing and marshalling of crowds of men and horses. The lines assigned to Joan are so simple and ingenuous that one is inclined to the belief that they were actually spoken by her and remembered by Gilles in collaborating with the unknown author of the play. We quote a charming *rondeau* which closes Joan's vision of the Archangel Michael.

ST. MICHEL

A Dieu, Jehanne, vraye pucelle
Qui est d'icelui bien aymée,
Ayez tousjours ferme pensée
De Dieu estre sa pastorelle.

PUCELLE

En mon Dieu, je vueil estre celle
De le servir, si lui agrée.

ST. MICHEL

A Dieu, Jehanne, vraye pucelle
Qui est d'icelui bien aymée.

PUCELLE

Mon bon seigneur, vostre nouvelle
De par moi sera reclamée
Au seigneur de ceste contrée
Pour la voye que dictes telle.

ST. MICHEL

A Dieu, Jehanne, vraye pucelle
Qui est d'icelui bien aymée,
Ayez tousjours ferme pensee
De Dieu estre sa pastorelle.

It seems odd, to put it mildly, that Gilles should attempt to reconstruct the main incidents of his association with Joan of Arc after his outburst of obscenity and murder. One would have thought that he would have shrunk from the attempt to awaken memories of Joan had we not the example of his action in wishing to commemorate the Holy Innocents while his hands, metaphorically speaking, were still red with their blood. No student of human abnormality could hope to keep pace with these lightning changes of mood. Their diametric inconsistency renders all hope of comprehension almost futile. So far as one can discover, there appears to have been some idea in Gilles' head of using the stage to vindicate the memory of Joan, but in all probability this consideration was only secondary to the urge of his own egotism, now degraded to a transpontine vanity.

The performances of the play, which continued for ten months, were free to the public, who came in their thousands from every part of France. Those who could not afford to leave their occupations were paid by Gilles to cover the loss of time spent at the theatre. Everyone had his appointed place, lords, bishops, and officers of the King.

" Seel pour sauf conduit de Gilles, sire de Reys er de Pousauges "

Entertaining was the order of the day and night, and huge crowds of admirers awaited Gilles at every turn and followed him from the theatre to the Croix d'Or, where he stayed with his personal staff. Largesse was scattered in profusion, and tables were set out where any one who could find a place supped at the expense of this new Haroun al-Raschid.

Gilles' household, imitating their master's prodigality, feasted their own special friends, and distributed favours on a scale befitting their position. History has no record of what the King thought of it all, but it may be imagined that his chief feeling was one of envy. Considering that he was denied credit and had to borrow right and left to meet his expenses, he must have wished that some of the money so recklessly squandered had found a way into his empty coffers. So far as Gilles was concerned it was his swan song. Like others since his day, he had to pay dearly for his patronage of the drama, and when the firework display died down he was faced with ruin.

CHAPTER VII

RUIN

It might seem incredible that anyone possessing the great wealth reputed to belong to Gilles de Rais could come to suffer financial embarrassment. From the various estimates of his fortune which have been given it is clear that Gilles was a millionaire many times over. The greater part of his possessions was represented by landed estates, and the first sign of insolvency was when his revenues no longer kept pace with his expenditure. The fabled wealth of a Midas could not have withstood the strain of Gilles' reckless spending. Orleans was merely an extraordinarily expensive item, but it was one of many such princely caprices, and their total effect was the inevitable one of completely drying up Gilles' liquid resources. Ever since he had opposed his grandfather and taken the bit between his teeth, money had been poured out, but the chief factor in his ruin was undoubtedly the avarice and dishonesty of his followers and hangers-on. The "*Mémoire des Héritiers,*" which was prepared after his death and presented to the King, as an attempt on the part of the heirs to recover the confiscated properties, says :

"The said Messire Gilles . . . by the inducement and council of certain of his servants and others who desired to enrich themselves with his wealth did take unto himself the government of all his lands and lordships . . . and so swayed by the falsity, craft and malice of his servants, that he did with them as he pleased without seeking the advice of his grandfather or listening to him further in any respect."

Many of his lesser estates had been mortgaged

to raise armies, but the bulk of his property was still intact. It was only a matter of time, however, until it was broken up and sacrificed for a shadow of its real value. The absence of a plentiful supply of ready money was intolerable to Gilles, and he commenced borrowing with a vengeance. Amongst the memoranda of Monsieur Doinel, a notary of Orleans, was a note which showed how hard Gilles had been hit. " Often the Lord de Rais put into the hands of buyers or lenders an object twice the value of the loan made to him. Sometimes it was rings and jewels of great price, that he either redeemed by their weight in gold or that he was obliged to abandon in the hands of the fortunate lender." When the proceeds of these pledges were exhausted, Gilles sent his retainers out armed with powers of attorney to negotiate loans and advances in his name. The documents which they carried, signed and sealed by Gilles, were used according to their discretion, or lack of discretion, as contracts and mortgages. The result of this indiscriminate trafficking was felt by Gilles' heirs long after his death.

The gold thus realised flowed through his hands. "When he received money, he distributed it amongst his pursuants, his stable boys, pages, grooms and people of low estate who used it for their profit and changed it into foolish pleasures." His capacity for raising money in Orleans was soon exhausted, and in October he moved to Montluçon, where for two months he lived at the Ecu de France. His hotel-keeper's bill amounted to 810 golden crowns, of which his distinguished guest could only pay 495 on account. Two of his servants were left behind as a pledge for the money. Gilles' haughty pride was outraged at the indignity of being hard up, and he proceeded to the extreme measure of breaking up his vast estates. An extract from the list of sales will indicate the extent of his operations.

"To Gauthier de Brussac, Captain-at-Arms, the towns and seigniories of Confolens, Chabannis, and Châteaumorant.

To Jean de Marsille, the Châtelaine, land and seigniories of Fontane-Melon in Anjou.

To Messire William de la Jumelière, the Château and lands of Blaison, of Chemillé in Anjou.

To Hardouin de Bueil, Bishop of Anjou, the land and seigniory of Grattecuisse, the Châtelaine and Château of Savény, half the forest of Brécilien.

To Messire Guy de la Roche-Guyon, the Château and lands of Motte-Achard and lands of Prigne, and of Maurière in Poitou.

To Jean de Malestroit, Bishop of Nantes, the Château and lands of Prigne, of Vuë, Bois-aux-Treaux in the parish of St. Michel-Sénéché, and "*un grand nombre de terres situées dans le clos du pays de Rais pour une somme énorme.*"

To William de Fresnière and Guillemont le Cesne, merchants of Anjou, the lands and seigniories of Ambières, St. Aubin de Fosse-Louvain in the province of Maine.

To Jean de Montecler, one of his men-at-arms, and to Guillemont le Cesne, aforesaid, the lands and seigniories of Voulte and Sénéché.

To Jean Rabateau, president of the parliament, the lands and seigniories of d'Auzence, de Clone and de Lyeon.

To William (apothecary of Poitiers), Jean Amère and Jacques de l'Epane, the lands Brueil—Mangon-lez-Portiers.

To George Tremoille (late favourite of the

King, now in retirement), twelve hundred *reaux* of gold on the rents of Champtocé to pay interest on twelve thousand *reaux* of gold borrowed from him.

To Perrenet Pain, burgess and merchant of Angers, such interest money on loans incurred on his land and seigniories.

To the Chapter of Notre Dame, Nantes, the Hôtel de la Suze.

To Jean le Ferron, St. Etienne de la Mer Morte . . ."

By this time Gilles' relations were up in arms against the dissipation of the family inheritance. They had tried peaceful persuasion, but when they learned of Gilles' intention to dispose of the revenues of Champtocé and Rais for the benefit of his Foundation of the Holy Innocents, they could no longer restrain themselves. It seemed to them that Gilles, not content to ruin himself, had decided to impoverish his heirs and successors for all time. A formal protest was made to the King. The prime movers in this matter were Dame Catherine, René de la Suze, and Guy de Laval, acting as the senior members of Gilles' house. All the details of Gilles' fortune and inheritance were set out in full, with an equally comprehensive statement of his riotous extravagance. The family's opinion of Gilles' religious display was expressed in a pungent phrase. "All this was nothing but vanity without devotion, and in defiance of good order."

Charles VII, by an Order in Council, took immediate steps to check his prodigal subject, and a royal interdict was issued prohibiting Gilles from selling or alienating further grounds, incomes or properties, and forbidding any person to contract sales or loans with him. The captains and guardians of all castles remaining to Gilles were warned under heavy penalties not to deliver any of these places to strangers, or suffer them to be delivered, until the Council of State had granted its consent. One effect of this measure was to put an end to Gilles' Foundation, all the beneficiaries being prevented by law from taking any part in the project. The interdict was proclaimed by a royal herald throughout all the territory belonging to Gilles which was subject to the King's writ.

Gilles was momentarily stunned by this drastic stroke, when unlooked for, though not disinterested, aid was offered by the Duke of Brittany. The Duke had long coveted Gilles' estates and had contemplated absorbing them into his own domain. Neither did he relish the King's attempt to interfere in what he regarded as a matter for his own jurisdiction. His son Peter was sent with an imposing escort to Niort-sur-Erdre to obtain the King's permission to continue his negotiations with Gilles for the remainder of his lands. Charles VII, stiffened by Richemont and Prégent de Coëtivy, refused to give way, and the Duke, in high dudgeon, thereupon swore that he would not allow the interdict to be published in any town in his Duchy. As a further act of petty spite he deprived his son-in-law and Gilles' cousin, Guy de Laval, who had served him with the interdict, of the office of Lieutenant-General of Brittany, and conferred the post upon Gilles. This cunning trick was intended to deceive Gilles to his real attitude. The Duke always tried to run with the hare and hunt with the hounds, and as a blind he gave letters to René of Anjou, pledging his sacred oath not to buy Champtocé or Ingrandes.

Despite this he entered into an agreement with Gilles in November, 1437, to secure these estates at bargain prices. In desperation, Gilles' relatives determined to prevent this transaction being carried out by wresting the two properties from Gilles' control. Armed with the King's authority, René de la Suze and Admiral Loheac, at the head of an armed company, seized Machecoul and Champtocé. For three months Gilles counter-attacked without success. The Duke meanwhile lay low in the hope that he would not be called upon to take sides, but when he was faced with the prospect of losing the estates which he had set his heart on, he boldly sent an army of his own to assist Gilles. Bribery of the guard rather than valour enabled the two forces to recapture the strongholds. The anger of the King fell upon Gilles for his open defiance of his fiat, and the recalcitrant nobleman was practically ostracised by being forbidden the Court.

This manifestation of the King's displeasure caused

Gilles little anxiety. He had broken too many laws to be disturbed by the enmity of Charles VII and his own relations. A more normal nature than his might have drawn strength from this chastening experience and submitted to the morally regenerating influence of his reverses, but the poison of excessive wealth and excessive pride had bitten too deep into Gilles' soul for any such healing process. Its only effect was to fill him with embittered defiance and an uncontrollable resolve to regain his power by any means. He had been too long in the fierce light of notoriety to be content with the shadow, and the sting of wounded pride tortured him. His one dominating idea was to restore his fallen fortunes, if possible to increase them a thousandfold, that he might wreak vengeance upon all the puny minds that had ventured to oppose him.

Catherine, his wife, made another attempt to

see him with regard to the future of their daughter Marie. Evidently she hoped that the consideration of the subject might be a means of bringing her husband to his senses. As on previous occasions he treated her ventures with indifference, and instructed Roger de Bricqueville to find a husband for his daughter. Nobody knew what Gilles' next move would be. He cut himself off finally from his family and entrenched himself at Tiffauges. Here he would be able to concentrate upon the problem of rehabilitating himself without interference of any kind. Gilles' intelligence could be exact and calculating when the need arose, and he strained it now to discover a way out of his difficulties. Clearly the enormous wealth he needed could not be acquired by any ordinary means. It was a problem almost beyond human solution, and the very difficulties it presented stirred Gilles' imagination to fever heat.

It was not without significance that Gilles de Rais, in answer to one of his friends, who had attempted to commiserate with him on his fallen fortunes, had said, "God could refuse nothing to a Laval, but if He did there is always the devil."

On the lips of the man who had outraged and murdered, such a statement could mean but one thing, that only from the principle and power of evil could he hope for aid.

CHAPTER VIII

BLACK MAGIC

The Château of Tiffauges is almost fifty miles from the grey city of Nantes. One leaves behind the soft Breton landscape and enters a world of sparse verdure, sterile and harsh. From the station of Torfu it is a distance of two miles, and as the village is approached there come into view the ruins of the stronghold of Gilles de Rais. The ravine of the Sèvre, with the river broad, deep and clear, splits the valley. The church of Notre Dame de l'Ascension stands on the very edge of the summit, but the eye is drawn irresistibly to the granite heights where the fortress which was Gilles' refuge, and the scene of his later crimes, stands out against the tyrannies of time.

Tiffauges was Gilles' favourite residence, no

doubt on account of its formidable walls, which rendered it impregnable against attack. He had come here to evolve the plan that was simmering in his brain; an idea as fantastic as all his thoughts, which at one stroke would give him the power of a demi-god. The idea was black magic and alchemy. Incongruous as this may sound to modern ears, it must be remembered that alchemy and occultism were subjects of vital import in Gilles' time. Those will-o'-the-wisps, the philosopher's stone and the elixir of life, were viewed as practical possibilities, and in the absence of anything approaching scientific data, there had grown up a belief that the quickest way to discovery lay through occult means.

Gilles had always been attracted by the hidden and mysterious. Saturated as he was with superstition and unbalanced by his sexual excesses and sanguinary crimes, the forbidden path of

Tower and Moat, Château of Tiffauges,
with a distant view of the Chapel of St. Vincent.

the hermetic art made an instant appeal to him. None had a better right than he to invoke the diabolic powers, which in this world at least he believed to be all-powerful. The bare idea of the course he proposed to follow stimulated him. Other men of learning and distinction dabbled in these things, but he would probe the mysteries of life and death to the core. A laboratory for his experiments, with vessels for distillation, retorts, alembics and all the paraphernalia of the mediæval wizard, was fitted up. The theory of the alchemist, put crudely, was that all substances were composed of one primitive matter which had as its basis mercury, freed from the four elements of earth, air, fire, and water. If the residue could be successfully treated with derivations of sulphur and arsenic, the philosopher's stone resulted.

This aspect of the subject was founded upon

certain metaphysical abstractions which, however vague and intangible, were free from the extravagances of black magic. Gilles de Rais viewed the problem from his own original and distorted standpoint. The axiom of the mystical school of alchemists, "What is above is as that which is below, and what is below is as that which is above," was by him given a sinister application. Likewise a saying of Paracelsus that in order to secure the *prima materia* it was only necessary "to mix and coagulate the rose-coloured blood of the lion and the gluten of the eagle," was regarded by Gilles as conveying an obscene meaning.

At the beginning his experiments were conducted single-handed until it became necessary to confide his ideas to his henchmen, Blanchet, Sillé and Bricqueville. He was still no more than a neophyte in black magic, and for all his physical courage he was strongly apprehensive of the hidden terrors of demonism. Attempts in the direction of the occult had only been tentative, and they had convinced him that he must find expert assistance for his further researches.

France at the time was overrun by charlatans, many of them Italians, who made the most extravagant claims. Gilles' first assistants were Antonio de Palermo, Cesare Rapparta, the Marquis de Ceva and Jean Petit, a Parisian goldsmith, and an impostor known as Jean de la Rivière, sometimes called " John the Englishman." Each experiment, with its inevitably inconclusive results, increased Gilles' anxiety until he had worked himself into a frenzy of suspense and anticipation. Days and nights on end, without eating or sleeping, were spent in the laboratory situated high up in the tower. There was one occasion when it seemed to the maddened Gilles that he was on the threshold of success.

The arrival of a mounted troop cut short further discoveries. It was the escort of the Dauphin, afterwards Louis XI, who had come to enlist the aid of Gilles against his father Charles VII. An ordinary experiment in alchemy would have provided a feature of interest for the royal visitor, but Gilles had surrounded himself with all the cabalistic signs and symbols of the forbidden rites. The unwelcome appearance of the Dauphin and the consequent risk of discovery threw Gilles into a panic, and he gave orders for the immediate destruction of all the apparatus. He was inconsolable after this, and turned to his Italians, who were bidden to amuse him with stories of orgies in the isle of Capri.

For an interval his heated imagination was transferred from science to vice. To restore his humour Bricqueville introduced a youth named Etienne Corrillaut as page and personal attendant to Gilles. Both the Rossignol and Griart still acted as confidential servants of the ordinary kind. For a spell Gilles relapsed into vice, and his quest of the philosopher's stone was momentarily set aside. Two other boys, Pierre and Perrinet Briant, were introduced to keep Corrillaut company. They were members of Gilles' choir, and took the place of the Rossignol in entertaining Gilles by hymn-singing. The intermission was a brief one. Day and night Gilles dreamed of what lay at the end of the experiments in alchemy. He was prepared to sacrifice everything but his soul, which he still regarded as capable of salvation, to find the key to omnipotence.

Eustache Blanchet had expressed the opinion that none of the necromancers at Tiffauges were equal to the task Gilles had imposed on them. The hint was sufficient to cause Gilles to despatch his emissaries everywhere to find fresh talent. Gilles de Sillé, after weeks of search, returned with the report that he had sent an evocator to Tiffauges, but that the man had been drowned in crossing a river, while another had died immediately on reaching Gilles' territory. Such ominous tidings aroused Gilles' superstitious fears, but his need of wealth overcame his qualms. Blanchet was sent to Italy with a letter of introduction from Anthony of Palermo to Giovanni di Fontanella, a doctor of Florence. The priest arrived in Florence in May, 1439, giving out that he was on business in connection with the Roman Court. Fontanella introduced him to an infamous set who had their headquarters at the house of Nicholas dei Medici. Ostensibly these gatherings were to discuss occult matters, but they included degenerates of every class, who were welcomed, irrespective of rank or wealth, into a fraternity bound together by their mutual interest in abnormal practices. They had agents in all the great capitals, which made it possible for them to exchange members and information.

The moving spirit of this clique was Francesco Prelati. Prelati was a young clerical student who had been seduced from his allegiance to the Church by the fascination of occultism. Originally a serious student of the pagan and oriental cults, he had become addicted to the vices peculiar to his set, until the occult had become nothing more than a cover for obscenity. Blanchet recognised in him at once the master of the black arts he had come to seek, and Prelati, influenced by the priest's account of the position of the Lord de Rais, agreed to accompany him to Tiffauges.

From the hour of his arrival, Prelati dominated Gilles de Rais. There existed a strange affinity between them ; Gilles conceived an instant affection for the young Italian, and their friendship was on a higher plane than Gilles' ordinary attachments. When asked at his trial why he loved Prelati, Gilles replied that he was "fascinated by his graciousness and charm, his intelligence and his elegant knowledge of Latin." Prelati's arrival was well-timed. Gilles' financial position had been greatly improved by the receipt of a large sum of money from the Duke of Brittany as part of the purchase price of Champtocé and Ingrandes. His enthusiasm was at white heat, and Blanchet's fraudulent reports of the marvels of which Prelati was capable had given his hopes a new lease of life.

Unconvincing as most of Prelati's attempts seem to have been, it is by no means certain that he did not succeed on several occasions in producing certain supernatural manifestations. As in modern spiritism one may find a grain of reality under a tissue of humbug, Prelati, whose chief idea was deception, surprised himself more than once by invoking his demons all too successfully. The first happening of this kind took place in the lower hall of the Castle. The devil-worshippers assembled at midnight, surrounded by all the trappings of the magic ritual. When everything was in readiness, Gilles entered the circle, but Gilles de Sillé, who was present, lost his nerve and refused to move a step. The fear spread to de Rais, who tried to make the sign of the Cross, but felt his hands paralysed. He then muttered the Alma Redemptoris, and immediately Prelati shrieked, " Out of the circle ! " The rest may be told in Gilles' own words :

"I heard voices which were not human and I became marvellously afraid. I left the evocator by himself, closing the door of the room upon him, whilst Gilles de Sillé fled by the window. But having come to the door to listen we heard that someone was beating the evocator, even as one might strike a feather bed. I drew my dagger and Gilles de Sillé did likewise; then we opened the door to see what was the matter, and the evocator was lying on the floor outside the circle, moaning and weeping and hurt exceedingly in the face and elsewhere, having a large bruise upon his forehead . . . and I feared he might die."

For seven days Prelati lay at the point of death, Gilles nursing him until he was restored to health. To the sceptic this incident will be regarded as fantastic mummery, but there is no aspect of psychic phenomena better authenticated than that which takes the form of " beating " by an invisible presence. It is related to *Poltergeist* activity, which is one of the most ordinary amongst such manifestations. At nearly all his *séances* Prelati tried to materialize a beautiful youth whom he named Barron, and for a long time he worked upon the imagination of Gilles by fanciful descriptions of the physical beauty of the demon who answered to this appellation. Gilles was as wax in the hands of Prelati, whose ingenious explanation for his many failures was that so long as Gilles continued any religious observances and carried pious objects on his person no tangible results would be forthcoming.

So interested had Gilles become in the business of demon evocation that he had almost lost sight of its original purpose. He relied upon Prelati to establish contact with the devil and from this source to find the secrets of his quest. If God worked miracles through his saints it was well known that the devil possessed great power and would assist those who did him homage. This was Gilles' reasoning, but so far the results were entirely negative. At this stage Prelati announced that the demons required greater proof of Gilles' loyalty and that nothing would move them but human sacrifice. Although Prelati was fully aware of Gilles' abnormalities, he had no knowledge of the murders committed at Champtocé and Machecoul. His request may have been intentionally designed on the supposition that Gilles would shrink from such extremes and consequently relieve him of the onus of failure. Whatever his motive, he was willing to go to the utmost limit to strengthen his hold on Gilles.

Strangely enough, the idea of offering a human holocaust to Satan stunned Gilles. It was not murder he feared, but devils. Prelati brushed aside his objections and Gilles was made to inscribe, with his own blood, a promise to immolate five children in honour of the devil. An indication of his mind is shown by the reservation which he added to the pledge that he should be " safe from harm both for his life and his soul." The idea that anyone might worship the power of evil and commit blasphemy and murder without detriment to the soul suggests, if nothing else, that Gilles' ratiocinative power was weakening. His spells and midnight *séances* had induced a state of neurosis which had left him a prey to every kind of fear. There was still reserved for him another chapter of horrors which make the most sanguinary monster of history seem mild in comparison.

CHAPTER IX

THE BEAST OF EXTERMINATION

The first two children chosen for the demoniac sacrifice were Jehan Barnard of Fort Launey and Jamet Brice of St. Etienne de Montluce. The victims had been found by Perrine Martin (La Meffraye)—a female accomplice working in conjunction with Blanchet—and the task of despatching the two children fell to Sillé. Gilles de Rais at no time required any incitement to slaughter, but to his warped mind murder for the satisfaction of lust was one thing and murder for the diabolic rites another. It became a question of degree, the one form of brutality appearing less culpable than the other. There is even some doubt whether Gilles took any active part in the blasphemous ceremonies conducted by Prelati in

CRYPT OF THE CHAPEL OF ST. VINCENT. CHÂTEAU OF TIFFAUGES, WHERE CHILDREN WERE SACRIFICED TO THE DEVIL.

the crypt of the chapel of St. Vincent, for the purpose of which the children were destroyed. At the back of his strange brain there seems to have lingered the hope that his soul would not be entirely blasted so long as he set some limit to his criminality. He was content to assume the guilt of the murders, leaving to Prelati the responsibility of propitiating the demons.

One day Etienne Corrillaut, the page, on entering his master's room, found Gilles holding a glass vessel containing the hands, heart and eyes of the children whom Sillé had butchered. Corrillaut was paralysed with fear, and Gilles was for having him put out of the way, but on the intervention of Bricqueville, who was present, his life was spared. Corrillaut was ordered to wrap the remains in white linen, and henceforth he became one of the murder gang. The sacrificial murders were associated by Gilles with the supernatural and called his "mysteries." He would fondle the heads of the decapitated children, kiss them in a frenzied transport, calling them his "dear angels," and exclaim: "Go, go pray to God for me."

The guileful and cold-blooded Prelati continued to buoy Gilles up with fresh promises of diabolic intervention. When Gilles displayed impatience or disappointment that the sacrifice had not brought any tangible return, Prelati contrived various impostures which, obvious though they were, succeeded in deceiving Gilles. It seems difficult to realise that the butchery, which sprang from Prelati's inspiration, could have been the result of anything so grotesque as the Italian's attempts to traffic with the devil. But the sight and smell of blood revived all Gilles' murder obsession. Just as at the beginning of his experiments in alchemy Gilles' interest in this mechanism obscured the end he had in view, so now murder in the interest of demonism induced a fresh outbreak of satyriasis. His burning desire to grasp power waned before the force of his blood-lust, until the five victims desired by Prelati had increased to the appalling total of one hundred and twenty. Two things stand out from this holocaust—the enormous scale on which the boys were trapped and the awful circumstances of their death.

Tiffauges in the early part of 1440 was an enclosed community of blood-stained perverts, to whom anything approaching normality would have seemed abnormal. On sifting the evidence, we find that at least eighteen of Gilles' household shared his complicity. The " Beast of Extermination " was no longer content to have his victims brought tamely to his presence, like innocents led to the slaughter. He preferred to organise " hunting " parties, which imparted to the dastardly business an element of " sport." The running down of the quarry heightened his zest and appealed to his satanic humour.

With Bricqueville and Sillé he made expeditions to the loneliest parts of the country, first marking his victim and then pouncing on it like a beast of prey. Young shepherds were his favourite quarry, as they were of another French murderer, Vacher, who four hundred and fifty years later (1888-1897) mutilated and killed eighteen peasant lads. Sometimes he varied the procedure by watching from a distance while his accomplices seized the unfortunate youth. If the boy struggled it was an added relish. Bound with ropes the boys were swung across the horses and at nightfall taken to the castle. Among those who aided de Rais in this detestable work were the woman Perrine Martin, who specialised in procuring children of tender years for sacrifice, cajoling them with promises of rich rewards if they entered the service of the Lord de Rais, and Corrillaut, who admitted to having secured thirty-six boys for the diabolic rites.

The methods of destruction employed were unspeakably revolting. According to Corrillaut's statement Gilles took a keen pleasure " in slaughtering boys, in watching them languish and die, and seeing their blood flow." One boy was bled to death that Gilles might wash his hands and beard in the warm blood. Other hideous details have been handed down to posterity. These butcheries were followed by spasms of remorse. At night Gilles would wander alone through the Château, pursued, as he thought, by the ghosts of his victims. In this state of mind he would fall on his knees in terrified repentance, swearing to God that he repented of his sins, and vowing to become a monk or go to the Holy Land on pilgrimage, begging his bread from door to door. On All Saints' Day we find him washing the feet of three poor men and serving them with food and drink. These moods were fleeting, and he returned to his savageries with renewed ferocity

An incident now happened which made it necessary for Gilles to hide the traces of his previous crimes at Champtocé and Machecoul. The Duke of Brittany had completed his final payments and was anxious to take possession of the castles. Gilles hastened to Champtocé and there began to remove the remains that had lain there for close on seven years.

Corrillaut and Robin Romulart, another of the Tiffauges gang, were entrusted with the unpleasant job of eliminating any record of the first murders. Sillé superintended the proceedings, and by his orders both men were lowered into the dry well into which the bodies had been flung. The decomposed remains were gathered into sacks in the charnel-house and hoisted to the surface. As the Duke's men were due to arrive on the following day, there was no time to be lost in disposing of the bodies. They were packed into large chests and taken during the night to a boat hidden amongst the willows at the river's edge. Sillé was for throwing the cargo into the Loire, but Gilles would not agree to this course. The boat was moored before reaching Nantes, and the bodies transferred to a cart and taken to Machecoul. Here the process of exhumation was repeated before the contents of the sacks were incinerated.

Corrillaut thus described the manner of disposing of the remains: " They were laid on a big andirons in the room of the Lord de Rais, with heavy pieces of wood, and placing on same dead bodies some dried faggots, they made a big fire, and putting fire to the clothes which burnt all, so that the bad smell was not noticed."

It is recorded that Gilles "struck his breast and cried to God for mercy" during this operation. Having become more composed, he gave orders for Mass to be sung for the repose of the souls of those whom he had done to death. This alternating sequence of crime and religious fervour is no proof that Gilles de Rais was subject to what is commonly called "religious mania." What it does, however, indicate quite clearly is that Gilles, despite the number of his crimes, could not escape from his conscience. It would be stupefied into seeming insensibility, but sooner or later he would be reminded of the penalty due from an avenging justice for his violation of every law, human and divine.

All this time Roger de Bricqueville had avoided taking any part in the proceedings. He appears to have had a prescience of danger, and desired to establish some kind of a case to show that he was not privy to the crimes. For this reason he secretly admitted two women, Dame de Jarville and Dame Chamin d'Avagouin, to witness the transfer of the bodies at Machecoul. Bricqueville professed to be as greatly shocked as the women at the discovery of what was going on, and counselled them to say nothing until he had investigated further. The task of burning the corpses was forced on the Rossignol, who contracted a fever as a result of the work and died.

When sufficient time had elapsed to allow Gilles to recover from his sham repentance, he went back to murder. From Machecoul to the

Maison de la Suze at Nantes he left a trail of blood. His journey to Nantes was ostensibly to conclude the sale of his mansion to the Cathedral Chapter, and during his stay in the town eleven additional murders were perpetrated. After Nantes came a visit to Vannes in July to secure some money from the Duke of Brittany, and negotiate the transfer of Bourgeneuf-en-Rais. Gilles had been invited to stay with the Duke, but he preferred the Lemoyne hostelry as offering greater freedom of action. Here at the lodgings of one of his attendants, André Buschet, who had decoyed the boy, Gilles committed another murder. The body was thrown into a drain and Corrillaut ordered to "push it out of sight." From Vannes Gilles accompanied the ducal retinue to Josselin, where Griart, now Gilles' chamberlain, succeeded in finding another victim to feed the monster's voracious appetite.

Gilles returned to Tiffauges satisfied with the financial results of his various transactions and confident of the Duke's friendship, but he did not stay there long. The old restlessness had caught him, and after a week or two of inactivity he left again with his personal staff on August 23 for Bourgeneuf-en-Rais. As the estate was now the property of the Duke, Gilles put up at the Grey Friars' Monastery, founded by one of the lords of Machecoul. He supped on the night of his arrival, which was St. Bartholomew's Eve, at the inn of Guillaume Rodigo, where he met a young student named Bernard le Camus. The boy was a native of Brest, where little French was spoken, and had been sent to Bourgeneuf-en-Rais to acquire the language. Corrillaut was given the hint to make friends with Camus and invite him to Gilles' apartments. Whatever inducement Corrillaut exercised, Camus, according to the deposition of Marguerite Sorin, chambermaid at the inn, slipped out " taking neither coat, shoes nor hood."

This was Gilles de Rais' last murder. Three weeks later, on September 13, he was arrested.

CHAPTER X

GILLES' ARREST

It frequently happens in modern murder cases that the discovery of the murderer is due to some secondary cause, or to circumstances not directly related to the actual crime. The uncovering of Gilles de Rais' guilt was effected by such means, and his arrest was brought about as a direct consequence of an act of sacrilege which he had committed.

The first hint that he was suspected came from Blanchet. While staying at Montaigne, a few miles from Tiffauges, the priest had heard rumours and hastened to warn Gilles. So strongly did Blanchet feel that the net was closing that he refused to return to Tiffauges and for a time hid himself in the outskirts of Machecoul. Gilles evidently attached no importance to the information, for beyond an attempt to bring Blanchet to the Castle, he gave little heed to the matter.

It would almost seem that there was a design in the coming retribution, for it was the Church whose teachings he had flaunted that was moving secretly against him. Jean de Malestroit, Bishop of Nantes, had heard the sinister allegations concerning Gilles, and at first was inclined to dismiss them as wild gossip. When the vague charges were supplemented by the disappearance of a nephew of the Prior of Chermère, who had been taken into the Rais household to be taught singing, he decided that there was at least a case for inquiry. The investigations filled him with grave disquiet, but there was still lacking sufficient direct evidence to warrant him bringing so serious a charge against a person of Gilles de Rais' eminence.

The Bishop commenced a series of episcopal visits over the areas from which the majority of the complaints had come. Wherever he went he was overwhelmed with revelations of Gilles' infamies. With the Church on their side the people were no longer afraid to speak plainly, and more than enough evidence was forthcoming to make out a *prima facie* case. To ensure that justice should be done all round the Bishop appointed deputy commissioners to gather plaints, sift evidence and make a record of all the depositions. While Jean de Malestroit hesitated through lack of evidence, founded neither on hearsay nor on surmise, on which to arraign Gilles de Rais, it was the murderer himself who enabled the Bishop to take decisive action.

In order to raise more money, Gilles de Rais had sold his property of St. Etienne de la Mer Morte, seven miles from Machecoul, to Geffroi

Le Ferron, whose brother Jean, a tonsured clerk, took possession from Gilles. Some difficulty had arisen about the completion of the purchase, and Gilles resolved to turn out Le Ferron and re-sell the property. Geffroi Le Ferron was treasurer to the Duke of Brittany, and was merely acting as intermediary. Gilles suspected that the Duke was trying to evade his obligations and cheat him out of the property. On Whit-Monday Gilles rode at the head of an armed force to settle accounts with Le Ferron. This was open revolt against the King and the Duke, who had jointly forbidden the levying of forces without special authority. Rival *seigneurs* had long taken advantage of the unsettled condition of the country to raid each other's estates and settle their private quarrels by an appeal to arms. To put an end to this state of affairs heavy penalties had been framed for such transgressions of the law.

Jean Le Ferron had left the Castle to assist at Mass almost at the same time that Gilles set out to attack him. Gilles surrounded the estate with troops and, taking a body-guard, forced his way into the church. The priest's communion had just finished and Gilles, wishing publicly to displace Le Ferron before the congregation, shouted aloud, "Ha, ribald, thou hast beaten my men and practised extortion on them, come out of the church or I will kill thee." The people scattered in terror, and Le Ferron was made a prisoner. Gilles marched him to the Castle and forced him to give orders for the surrender of the garrison. The Duke replied to this challenge by sending his sergeant-general and another of his officials to remonstrate with Gilles, who promptly seized both and placed them under arrest. Jean was furious at this open affront to his authority. He immediately declared Gilles a rebel, and ordered the Count de Richemont to proceed against his recalcitrant subject. Arthur de Richemont had not forgotten Gilles' good offices in getting him reinstated in the royal favour, and he was loth to take action which he knew might lead to Gilles' ruin. Instead of using force, he persuaded Gilles to release the Duke's servitors, and followed this by patching up the quarrel between the two.

Gilles was in high fettle, but he had not reckoned with the Church. Now that he had violated one of its most jealously guarded privileges, the inviolability of its clergy, the Bishop was provided with a most powerful weapon against Gilles. If he wanted any further incentive to pursue him it was supplied by Richemont's action in settling the dispute. Richemont was an old enemy of the Bishop, whom no one notable occasion he had thrown into prison on a charge of conspiring with the English. If the Bishop could prove that Gilles was a murderer he would be able to hit back at Richemont, and this very human desire to pay off old scores increased his eagerness to secure a conviction. He made strong representations to the Duke that Gilles should not go unpunished, and redoubled his efforts to make the case for the prosecution more complete.

On July 30, 1440, while Gilles, all unsuspecting of the blow that was about to fall, was murdering a boy at Vannes, the Bishop felt that the moment had arrived in which to show his hand. A formal indictment or "Declaration of Infamy" was put on record. Apparently it was the first step made publicly against Gilles de Rais, as it is the first paper forming part of the ecclesiastical record in the archives of the Department of the Loire Inférieure.

Armed with the testamentary proof of Gilles' guilt, the Bishop laid his case before the authorities. Apart from the weight of evidence with which he confronted the Duke, the Bishop had forwarded all the documents dealing with the charges to the King's representatives. By so doing, he had ensured action by the State, and provided against the contingency of Gilles' rank and position defeating the ends of justice. Such a precaution also ensured against any attempt on the Duke's part to hamper the prosecution. On this point, however, the Bishop had misread the Duke of Brittany's mind. The arrest and prosecution of Gilles de Rais meant, so far as the Duke was concerned, that Gilles would be prevented from redeeming his properties according to the terms of the agreement, which stipulated that this could be undertaken within a period of six years. Gilles was doubly doomed by the plain evidence of his

CHAPEL OF ST. VINCENT, CHÂTEAU OF TIFFAUGES, AT THE PRESENT DAY.

crimes, and by the financial intrigues and petty spites of his enemies.

News of the storm that was brewing reached Gilles de Rais at Machecoul, and spread panic amongst his accomplices. Gilles alone seemed to be unmoved, and watched their flight with a stoical calm. To him it was the last act of the drama of his life, and instinctively he felt that nothing could stop the march of Fate. There was a certain dignity in his composure, contrasted with the terror-stricken attitude of his fellow-degenerates. Sillé and Bricqueville led the way. Prelati, relying upon his cunning, and thinking he would avert suspicion if he remained in Machecoul, moved from the Castle to a poor quarter of the town, where he shared rooms with Blanchet. The only two who remained at Gilles' side were Corrillaut and Griart, although he had pointed out that they must think of themselves and not consider his danger. Gilles could not hide from himself that his course was run, but he still hoped against hope that his relationship to the Duke of Brittany might save him.

There were three alternatives before him. He could resist arrest, fly the country, or submit. The first would have been a tacit admission of his guilt and would have raised all the powers of the kingdom against him. Flight meant the same thing, with the added disadvantage of having to leave behind what remained of his fortune. He decided to accept his fate and trust to his star.

The actual arrest proceeded smoothly. On September 13, Jean l'Abbé, a captain of the Duke's army, and a company of soldiers presented themselves at Machecoul. Gilles received his captors with unconcern. "This is the moment I go to God," was his cynical remark. "I often wished to become a monk, and here is l'Abbé, under whom I must engage myself." When he saw that his pose was ineffective, he became serious and, shrugging his shoulders, said, "No human power can prevent the will of Heaven from being accomplished." The usher of the Ecclesiastical Court then handed Gilles the process. On being told that it was a citation to appear before the Bishops' tribunal, Gilles, in his lordly manner, ordered some gold pieces to be given to the official for his trouble. A search of the Castle followed, and the carbonised remains of the youth, Bernard Le Camus, together with a blood-soaked shirt, were discovered.

Gilles, with Corrillaut and Griart, was then formally arrested and taken the same evening to Nantes. The whole city was throbbing with excitement at the news. Thousands had assembled to see Gilles, Lord of Rais, Lieutenant-General of Brittany, Counsellor of the King and Marshal of France, led with his two companions in chains and confined in the tower of the Castle of Nantes.

CHAPTER XI

THE TRIAL

GILLES was lodged in an upper room of the Castle, comfortable and well lighted, where he was accorded all the privileges due to a prisoner whose guilt had yet to be confirmed. The methods of the prosecution conducted by the Bishop of Nantes would have commended themselves to any modern judicial authority.

There were two tribunals appointed to sit in judgment, the Ecclesiastical Court, presided over by Jean de Malestroit, and the Civil Court, with Pierre de l'Hôpital as its head. As the charges upon which Gilles had been arrested came primarily within the jurisdiction of the Ecclesiastical Court, its findings would necessarily guide the action of the Civil tribunal.

After six days' confinement, Gilles was summoned to attend a preliminary examination in the large Hall of the Tour Neuve. He heard the act of accusation read, and boasted that he was quite ready to prove his innocence. So far his manner was tranquil and he treated the whole matter lightly—refusing even to avail himself of his right to establish, if he could, a defence. His confidence was inspired by the circumstance that the indictment had confined itself to the crimes of heresy and sacrilege. These were offences which did not call for any extreme penalty, and for which he could make reparation without any loss of prestige. In the interval of adjournment he spent most of his time hearing Mass, for which permission had been given. One of the priests of his own household was allowed to officiate, but he was pledged not to admit Gilles to the sacraments.

A very unpleasant surprise, however, was in

store for Gilles. The Bishop of Nantes had been awaiting the result of an independent inquiry set up by the Civil Court, and now that this had firmly established his action, the act of accusation had been widened to admit the charges of murder and offences against nature.

When Gilles was again confronted by the Ecclesiastical Commissioners, on October 8, he was aghast at the new development. He quickly determined that the prosecution should not have it all their own way, and in his most arrogant and contemptuous manner he demanded that he should be tried by his peers. The Bishops overruled his plea as being frivolous, and reminded him that Church and State alone, and not the culprit, had the power to appoint judges. Gilles was informed that he would be called upon to make a formal appearance before the Civil Court in three days' time, and the session was adjourned for the day. The members of the tribunal then retired for refreshment, custom requiring that they should fast from sunset of the previous evening, so that their minds might be clear when they came to the hall of judgment.

All Gilles' wits were taxed to discover the best means of meeting this fresh, but not wholly unexpected, emergency. Should he admit his guilt and throw himself on the mercy of his judges, or trust to his rank and position, and a brazen denial of the charges, to carry him through ? The quandary was complicated by his uncertainty as to how much his judges really knew.

On October 11, when he appeared before the Civil Court at the Palace of La Bouffey, his mind fluctuated in the most uncertain way. Ultimately he gambled on an extreme course, which would, he thought, show him at his best without definitely revealing his guilt. He commenced by requesting, in his most authoritative manner, that the proceedings should be expedited as much as possible, as he was anxious to dedicate himself to the service of God. Before the Court had recovered from its surprise, he followed this statement up by declaring that it was his intention to bestow large monetary gifts on the church in Nantes and give the greater part of his belongings to the poor. If Gilles hoped to hoodwink justice by this pretence of charity, he was grievously disappointed. The President's reply was that "if it were right that he should think of his soul, it was necessary that he should satisfy the justice of man as well as the justice of God."

Two days later there was another sitting of the Ecclesiastical Court, which was now fully constituted to carry out the trial and pronounce judgment. The Promoter of the case, an office analogous to that of Public Prosecutor, was

Guillaume Chapeillion, a priest of the Church of St. Nicholas of Nantes, and the judges were the Bishop of Nantes—President—and the Bishops of Le Mans, St. Lo and St. Brieuc. Pierre de l'Hôpital was in attendance as the representative of the secular authorities.

As in a present day *cause célèbre*, public excitement ran high, and the Court and its approaches were crowded with spectators anxious to catch a glimpse of the prisoner. The opportunity for dramatic effect was too good to be lost on Gilles. Although his life was at stake, he intended to make the most of the occasion by a carefully prepared appearance. He entered the Court amidst a suppressed hum, which changed to a tense silence as the Lord de Rais, holding his head high, faced the judges. Gilles was attired in white, doubtless with the idea of symbolising his innocence. He wore tight-fitting hose, a shirt and vest of white silk, and white boots. His doublet was of pearl grey silk, embroidered with gold stars, and his chapel or round cap had a bordering of ermine, a decoration which only the great feudatories of Brittany were privileged to wear. A sash of scarlet was about his waist, from which hung a poignard in a red velvet sheath. On his breast were displayed all his military and seigniorial orders, and from his neck was suspended a chain of gold and a reliquary.

The proceedings were opened by a recital of the charges, which consisted of forty-nine articles, and stigmatised Gilles as "a heretic, an apostate, a sodomist, and a violator of the immunities of the Church." To satisfy justice, the Prosecutor appealed to the judges to punish and excommunicate the prisoner, in accordance with the laws of Church and State. The crowded court had listened to the arraignment with feelings of amazement and incredulity, and now every eye was turned towards Gilles de Rais to hear his answer to the charges. All Gilles' composure had deserted him. He stood white and trembling, evidently at a loss for words to reply to the Prosecutor's attack. Suddenly a tornado of abuse escaped from his lips He declared that it was a humiliation for one of his degree to appear before a Court of "simoniacs and ribalds," and that he would rather be hanged by the neck than have any dealings with them Then, appealing to Pierre de L'Hôpital, he said: "I am astonished that you should allow ecclesiastical judges to accuse me of such infamies."

Chapeillion conducted the case for the prosecution vigorously, never once losing his temper despite the prisoner's outbursts. As Gilles persisted in his denials, shouting down and fighting the judges, the Court declared him "manifestly contumacious," and proceeded to excommunicate by writ and public sentence.

There was a further adjournment of two days, and on Gilles' reappearance both judges and public had another surprise. All his bluster and bravado were gone, and he who had been all defiance now submitted to the jurisdiction of the Court, which before he had scornfully rejected, and entreated pardon for his violence. His gay attire had been exchanged for sober garments, and he kept his eyes downcast. The Bishop of Nantes, seeing in this a change of heart, spoke gently to the prisoner, who, when again asked if he recognised the jurisdiction of the Court, assented. Whilst Gilles was being sworn, an officer arrived having in custody Corrillaut, Prelati, Griart and Blanchet, in addition to La Meffraye and Théophanie Blanchu. Gilles declined to question his associates, stating that he would rely upon their truthfulness and on the justice of the Court. The witnesses were afterwards removed for private interrogation by the *greffiers* in accordance with usage.

Scarcely had they left the Court when Gilles, to the astonishment of all, fell upon his knees weeping and entreating the Bishop to remove the ban of excommunication. There were murmurs of sympathy from the densely packed Court, and Jean de Malestroit, convinced of Gilles' repentance, agreed to accede to his wish. Prelati's statement was then read, and Gilles, asked if he had anything to say, replied in the negative. To every question he offered the same blank denial.

The judges were in a dilemma. Instead of calling witness and hearing verbal testimony, as would be done to-day, the prosecution relied upon the sworn depositions of Gilles' accomplices, and of all who had any knowledge relevant to the crime. An enormous amount of evidence had thus been accumulated from various sources, but the procedure of the Court was that the prisoner should admit the truth before a decision could be formulated. Gilles' denial of every count in the accusation was equivalent to a plea of not guilty, but unfortunately for him he was unable to substantiate his assumption of innocence, and at the preliminary investigations he had refused to take the oath. All this had set up a distinctly unfavourable impression, and his judges may be forgiven for believing that he was attempting to trifle with the course of justice. In order to escape from this *impasse*, the promoter applied to the judges that the prisoner might be subjected to torture. The application was referred to the assessors, who pronounced in favour of the request.

This was enough for Gilles, who at once offered to confess. It was eloquent of his failing courage that he stipulated for his admission to be heard far from the torture chamber. At two o'clock in the afternoon, in the presence of the Bishop of St. Brieuc and Pierre de l'Hôpital, Gilles made a confession of his crime. When he had finished speaking, Pierre de l'Hôpital asked: "Who gave to you, and how did you get the idea of committing these crimes?"

"No one," Gilles answered. "My own imagination drove me to do so. The thought was my own, and I have nothing to which I attribute it, except my own desire for the knowledge of evil."

This reply did not satisfy his questioner, who pressed him to be more exact. Gilles was racked by the shame of his disclosures and anxious to end the ordeal. "Alas, *Monseigneur*," he protested, "you torment yourself and me also, both of us unnecessarily."

"No," responded the President, "I do not torment myself, but I am astonished at what you have said, and I am scarcely content with it. My only desire is to have you tell the truth concerning the cause."

Gilles' self-control was on the point of breaking down, and his voice and manner were that of a man labouring under great distress.

"There is no other cause," he cried impatiently; "I have told you the truth and everything as it happened. . . . I have said to you all things as they are, and enough to kill ten thousand men."

When Prelati was brought in to corroborate his statements Gilles had a fit of weeping and, embracing his former accomplice, said: "Farewell, François, my friend. We shall never more see each other in this world. I pray God that He may give you good patience and knowledge, and rest assured that if you . . . trust in God we shall see each other again amidst the great joys of Paradise."

This confession of Gilles was termed *extrajudiciaire*, and the next day he was called upon to repeat and confirm his previous statement, supplementing it by any details that it lacked. The latter was the judicial confession, and when it was completed the prisoner was ordered to read it publicly in Court. No greater humiliation could have been imposed on the once proud and mighty Lord de Rais, and he spent the night praying for strength to sustain him.

A densely packed Court awaited the culmination of the trial. This was arranged for the following day. Gilles was led in looking haggard and drawn, his pallor heightened by the black damask pourpoint and hood of black velvet which he wore. Enjoined by the prosecutor to proclaim his guilt, he began the recital of his crimes in a voice that trembled. It was a terrible ordeal, but he held himself for the task, sparing neither himself nor his hearers any of the revolting details. His implacable murders and violations, the agonies of his victims, all were described unsparingly. The auditors held their breath, until the frozen silence of the court was shattered by the piercing scream of a woman, perhaps the mother of one of the murdered boys. Even the priests and judges, their nerves tempered by the fires of the confessional, shuddered as they listened to the hoarse voice describing unimaginable bestialities.

Then a startling incident happened, which thrilled the Court and turned Gilles' face grey and wet with perspiration. At the grossest part of the narrative the Bishop of Nantes rose quickly from his seat and, moving towards the crucifix that hung above the judges' tribune, veiled the face of the Redeemer. Nothing more was wanted to complete Gilles' agony or remorse, and in a passionate outburst he cried between his sobs : " Oh, God, my Redeemer, I ask pardon and mercy ! " He looked towards the gaping spectators with the words : " Oh ! parents of those innocents I have cruelly murdered, I beg the charity of your prayers."

Another impressive moment followed. The Bishop of Nantes embraced the prisoner, saying : " Pray that the anger of the Most High may be pacified and that your contrite tears may purify the soul of your being." When Gilles had regained his tranquillity, he turned to the crowd and said in a steady voice :

" If I have so much offended against God, I owe it, alas, to the evil direction that I received in my youth. I went, at the time, the reins upon my neck free to pursue all my pleasures, and I did not refrain myself from anything evil.... Judged by the declaration that I have made here, of the faults of which I am capable, by the shame that appears on my face, I hope to obtain more easily the grace of God and the remission of my sins. I think they will be easier forgotten in His mercy. My entire youth was passed in the delicacies of the table, I was subject to my caprices, nothing to me was sacred, all the evil that I could do has been accomplished. In this I put all my hopes, all my thoughts, all my cares, everything that was prohibited. There was no means, however shameful and disgraceful, that I was not ready to employ.... Whatever may be the perils of my soul, I am still not drowned or lost—I am redeemable and I believe that the clemencies of God and the suffrages of Holy Church ... have succoured me with much mercy."

Everybody, moved by a common impulse, knelt to pray. The verdict of the Ecclesiastical tribunal that Gilles was "shamefully guilty" was then put on record, but the pronouncement of the capital sentence was left to the discretion of the Civil Court, to which this prerogative belonged. Whilst the trial was proceeding Griart and Corrillaut, whose offences were matters for the secular authorities alone, had been sentenced to death.

That same evening Gilles was removed to Bouffay for sentence. To prove its independence as a separately constituted tribunal, and that it was not unduly biased by what had already taken place, the Court appointed an advocate, Henri Méchinot, to plead on Gilles' behalf. The prisoner himself remained in his room aloof from the proceedings, absorbed in his Book of Hours, one of the gems of his library.

The mediæval lawyer who defended Gilles

was faced with a hopeless task, but in his address he displayed an acumen and understanding of the psychological factors which were quite remarkable. He pictured his client " invaded by pride and other demons who, well armed and resolute, had assailed his fortress and enlisted it by force, even as the Greeks coming forth from the wooden horse did invade the unhappy city of King Priamus. Messire de Rais could not be accounted guilty of the excesses committed by pride and his band, for a city taken by assault was innocent of the depravity, pillaging and cruelty to which it was subjected by its tyrants and unjust possessors."

Instinctively the lawyer had arrived at the same conclusion as the modern psychologist. Stripped of its hyperbole, the pleading was a piece of sound deductive reasoning, but the death penalty was a foregone conclusion, and the verdict of the

Court was unanimous. Not all the judges were agreed as to the manner in which the sentence should be carried out, and this was debated at considerable length. Some favoured decapitation, but finally general agreement was reached that Gilles should be hanged and burned before death ensued, "the sentence to be carried out on the morrow at eleven o'clock."

Gilles received the news of his doom quietly, and thanked Pierre de l'Hôpital for having notified him of the exact hour of his execution.

"Since," he said, "Griart and Corrillaut, my servants, and I have together committed enormous and frightful crimes, may it please you, my lord, that we may suffer the penalty together and that we may be executed at the same time. I am the cause and beginning of their fall. I can sustain death and speak to them of their salvation at the moment of passing. I can expressly show them the example to die well, for if it is otherwise, if my servants do not see me die, if they imagine that I remain unpunished, I, the cause of all their crime, they may fall into despair. Give me this favour, for I hope by the grace of Our Lord that, after having been the cause of their fall, I shall by my words and example be the cause of their salvation."

This was granted, and, as a reward for Gilles' spirit of repentance, it was decided that his body should not be reduced to ashes, but taken from the flames before being consumed and buried in whatever church in the town of Nantes the condemned man should choose. Gilles asked that his remains should rest in the Carmelite Church, and as a further favour, that the President would beg of the Bishop of Nantes to order a general procession of the people to pray for the repose of his soul at the moment of execution.

CHAPTER XII

THE END

On the morning of Gilles de Rais' execution—Wednesday, October 26, 1440—a solemn procession went through the streets at nine o'clock praying for Gilles and his accomplices, in compliance with the last wish he had expressed. From his cell the prisoner could hear the waves of sound, as monks, nuns, priests, merchants and nobles filed out of the churches chanting the penitential psalms. An enormous gathering, which included the Duke of Brittany and his suite, had gathered in the meadow of La Madeleine, near the present site of the Hôtel Dieu, where three gibbets and pyres had been prepared.

Gilles, Griart and Corrillaut were brought

from their cells under a strong guard and marched to the place of execution. The way taken enabled Gilles to cast a look at his Hôtel de la Suze, the scene of many great gatherings and of some of his worst crimes. His thoughts were of his approaching end, and he prayed incessantly until he stood underneath the gibbet. There were a few moments left to Gilles while the final preparations were made, and he utilised them to encourage Griart and Corrillaut. The huge crowd surged forward to catch the moralising of the man who had broken every moral law.

"There is not so great a sin," Gilles said, "that man can commit that God in His paternal goodness and benignity will not pardon, if only the sinner has great repentance and contrition in his heart, and he asks forgiveness with good hope. God is readier to pardon than the sinner is to ask. Thank God for showing us a manifest sign of his mercy in allowing us to die in our force and good memory, instead of punishing us suddenly for our evil deeds. Have such a regret for your crimes that you do not fear death, which is such a little thing, and without which we can not see God and His glory. How much ought we to wish to be out of this world where there is only misery. . . . Together we have sinned, and immediately our souls are separated from our bodies we shall meet with God in Paradise."

Griart and Corrillaut in their turn assured their master that they "held the death of this world very agreeable for the great desire and confidence they had in God's mercy."

Gilles knelt down and prayed, and then, turning to the crowd, said: "I am your Christian brother. Oh, all of you who hear me, especially you whose children I have killed, by the Passion

EXECUTION OF GILLES DE RAIS
From a Miniature
(*Manus. franc.* 23836, *Bibl. Nat.*)

of Our Lord I beg of you to pray for me. With all your hearts forgive me the ill I have done you, as you yourself desire pardon and mercy from God." Then he commended his soul to Saint James and Saint Michael, whose intercession Joan of Arc had asked at her death.

Gilles was the first of the three to pay the penalty. The rope was placed round his neck, while one of the executioners stood ready to kindle the fire. Griart and Corrillaut shouted their encouragement to Gilles to die as "a strong and valiant knight." At the same moment the steps on which Gilles stood were drawn from under him and the flames of the pyre curled round the half-strangled figure. When it was seen that the fire had completed the work of the gibbet, the remains were taken from the flames and given over to some members of the Rais family, who were waiting in readiness.

The body was conveyed to the Carmelite Church and placed in a specially prepared vault.

Griart and Corrillaut, like Gilles, met their fate with fortitude. The impression produced by the execution was so great that large numbers of people fasted for three days to secure the spiritual deliverance of the criminals. There were no more fervent supplications than those which came from the parents of the children who had been done to death. Gilles' place of sepulture seems to have been chosen by him not only from its pious associations, but with a view to blotting out the memory of his dishonour. The Church of the Carmelites was the spot where reposed all who were illustrious in name and virtue. There lay the ancient Dukes of Brittany and their consorts. The heart of the Duchess Anne (the last Duchess of Brittany) was buried there between her father and mother.

A monument in the form of a Calvary was raised on the place where Gilles expiated his crimes by his daughter Marie. A fragment of this is still preserved in the Archæological Museum of Nantes. Up to the time of the Revolution it was a place of pilgrimage where mothers and nurses came to pray to the Bonne Vierge de Crée-Lait. During the Terror the Carmelite Church was demolished by fire, the tombs, sculptured by Michael Colomb, were broken and the remains scattered to the four winds.

Of the fate of Gilles' remaining accomplices few details are known. His two principal henchmen, Gilles de Sillé and Roger de Bricqueville, fared incomparably better than they deserved. Sillé, as we know, disappeared at the first sign of danger and succeeded in escaping from France. Bricqueville remained in hiding for many years, and in 1456 he petitioned the King to grant him letters of remission cancelling any punishment attached to his share of the crime. The reasons advanced for seeking the royal clemency were that he had little sense or understanding at the time he entered Gilles de Rais' service, and that he stood in great fear of his kinsman. He made much of the patriotism of his family and of his own war service against the English, and in the end the King was persuaded to cancel whatever punishment might be due to him in the matter. The men-at-arms, chaplains, servants and choir-boys who made up Gilles' entourage were sent about their business by his widow, who saw in this host of parasites one of the causes of her husband's ruin. A year after Gilles' death she married Jean de Vendôme, and the son of their marriage inherited Tiffauges, which remained in their family until 1560. Nearly two hundred years later the castle became the property of the Marquis de la Bretesche. The present Marquis occupies a comparatively modern château a short distance from the old stronghold of Gilles de Rais.

The luck of his master the devil for a time followed François Prelati. He was condemned to perpetual imprisonment, but by some device managed to escape. Undaunted by his past experience, he sought for another noble patron and found him in the person of René, King of Anjou, who, like Gilles de Rais, was interested in the transmutation of metals. Prelati succeeded in getting himself appointed to the captainship of La Roche-sur-Yon, but, not satisfied with this, he had had the imprudence to seize a treasurer of France and hold him to ransom. The Grand Council got hold of the matter, and Prelati's true indentity was revealed. He was condemned to death and executed on May 2, 1456.

Within a short period of Gilles' execution an attempt was made by his family to lessen the taint surrounding their name. Reference has already been made to the "*Mémoire des Héritiers.*" This was drawn up and presented to the King and the Duke of Brittany with the object of proving that Gilles de Rais was mad and consequently that all contracts of sale and mortgage were null and void. It failed in its purpose, but some time later Prégent de Coëtivy, the husband of Marie de Rais, once more tried to re-open the issue. He had great influence with the King, whom he induced to believe that Gilles was the victim of a miscarriage of justice. Letters patent were prepared calling upon the Duke of Brittany, Pierre de l'Hôpital and the Bishop of Nantes to appear before the constituted authority and justify their action.

In this curious document the King speaks of

Gilles de Rais as having been "unduly and without cause condemned to death and made to die." Some commentators have regarded this as a strong presumption that Gilles was innocent, whereas it is merely one of the many evidences in existence that the King was half mad. Furthermore, the royal citation was never issued, and therefore may be looked upon as nothing more than an irresponsible move in favour of the financial claims of Prégent de Coëtivy. When he died, after failing in his endeavours to rescue the Rais properties, his relations seized Champtocé. To defend herself against the cupidity of his family Marie de Rais married a second time, her choice falling on her cousin André de Laval, Admiral, and companion-in-arms of her father.

Of the many attempts made to rehabilitate Gilles de Rais, the most notable are the works of Jewish writers. M. Salomon Reinach, when the Dreyfus affair was under discussion, tried to demonstrate that the evidence against Gilles was unreliable. The late Mr. Andrew Lang, in "The Maid of Orleans," quotes Reinach with approval and finds some similarity between the actions of Joan's accusers and the tribunals which convicted Gilles de Rais. The one point in Reinach's argument worthy of consideration is the very obvious one that Gilles only confessed to his crimes under the threat of torture.

Against this there is the abundant evidence of his accomplices, and of witnesses who had no possible reason for lying. It is quite untenable that both the civil and religious Courts conspired to punish an innocent man, and that all the complainants and witnesses committed perjury. There is no analogy whatever between the trial of Gilles de Rais and the persecution of Joan of Arc, and it would be grotesque to seek for one. Reinach's thesis has been riddled by Canon Dourville, who has shown that texts have been distorted to suit the purpose of the author. Another futile endeavour is that of Dr. Ludovico Hernandez in his "*Procès Inquisitorial de Gilles de Rais.*" Dr. Hernandez suggests that the Bishop of Nantes was in the pay of the English, and on this assumption, which has no relevance to the matter, asks us to discount the action of Jean de Malestroit in bringing Gilles de Rais to justice. Even allowing for the possibility of political motives being mixed up with the currents and cross-currents which Gilles' prosecution aroused, this suggestion can have no bearing on Gilles' guilt. Dr. Hernandez' other arguments are equally worthless. He is astonished that none of the remains of the murdered children were produced at the trial, although we have it clearly stated by Gilles and his servitors that all the evidences of their crimes were destroyed. The modern defenders of Gilles put forward reasons equally flimsy for their belief, but at least they have the merit of being original and almost romantic. They claim that a seam of gold ran under the Castle of Machecoul, and therefore there was no need for Gilles to indulge in alchemy and demonism in order to raise the wind. One is at a loss to know the source of their information. It would have been more to the point had any of these attempts to whitewash Gilles concerned themselves with his attitude during the trial.

It it were possible to dismiss Gilles' own confession, or even to depreciate it on account of the manner in which it was extorted, if it were possible also to ignore the weighty mass of evidence and the absence of any sound motive for hunting a guiltless man to his doom, one might find room for doubt in Gilles' extraordinary display of religious fervour. Were these passionate cries to God the actions of a guilty man? Was it possible for anyone possessing so profound a religious sense as these indicated to be capable of the acts for which he was convicted? Here at all events there was sincerity, in striking contrast to his former religious ebulliency. The chief paradox of Gilles' life, and the main difficulty of any effort to unravel it, is that undoubtedly he did possess a deep consciousness of the supernatural, but withal he was completely unmoral. Superficially this may seem irreconcilable, but it is by no means so uncommon a phenomenon as it seems. Religion and morality are not always the same, and in Gilles' case the one bore but a distant relation to the other. Gilles' parade of religion was not that of the common hypocrite. Not all his vice or murders could eliminate his longing for the supernatural, and nothing affected him more deeply than being excommunicated. So long as he could maintain any form of contact with his Church he felt that he was not entirely lost His striking phrase "I am redeemable" shows that he had always preserved this religious sense. The power was lacking to translate it into a standard of life, and in the disparity we have the explanation for all the inconsistencies and contradictions that made his life a tragedy.

The Abbé Bossard, in his scholarly work, the result of a thorough analysis of all the documentary evidence, leaves no room for doubt in the question of Gilles de Rais' guilt. Likewise Emile Gabory, the curator of the Archives at Nantes, and the foremost living authority on the history of Gilles de Rais, to whom we are under many obligations, ridicules all these vain attempts to turn black into white.

APPENDIX I

GENEALOGY OF GILLES DE RAIS.

I. HOUSE OF LAVAL.

Guy de Montmorency (sixth of the name, called de Laval, younger son of Mathieu II, Seigneur of Montmorency and Constable of France).

- Guy de Laval VII.
- Guy de Laval VIII.
- Guy de Laval IX. Foulques de Laval, *m.* Jeanne de Rais (called Jeanne la Folle) (*d.* 1358).

Junior Branch.

Guy de Laval (called Brumor).
m. (1) Jeanne de Montmorency.
(2) Tiphaine (d. of Chevalier de Husson and niece of Bertrand du Guesclin).

Guy de Laval, de Rais (*d.* 1415) adopted by Jeanne de Rais, La Sage (See Table II).
m. Marie de Craon.

- Gilles de Rais (1404-1440) *m.* Catherine de Thouars.
- Marie de Rais, *m.* (1) Prégent de Coëtivy, Admiral of France, later Baron de Rais. (2) André de Laval, Seigneur of Loheac, Admiral and Marshal of France (No issue).

- René de la Suze (*d.* 1474). *m.* Anne de Champagne.
- Jeanne de Laval, *m.* François de Chauvigny, Prince of Déols.
- André de Chauvigny, Prince of Déols (*d.* 1520 without issue).

199

II. HOUSE OF RAIS (*Ancient Branch*).

Garsire (*ca.* 1161).

Harcourt or Arcoit (*d.* 1190).

Garsire or Garsile (*d.* 1225).

Raoul (*d.* 1248) *m.* Françoise Salvagie de la Motte-Achard.

Eustachie, *m.* Girard Chabot, br. of Thibaud Chabot, Lord of Aulnes and Rocheservière.

New Line.
Godefroy, Seigneur of La Maurière

— Girard Chabot II. *m.* (2) Jeanne de Craon, also (1) Emme de Chateaugonthier and (3) Marguerite des Barres.

— Eustachie, *m.* Gérard de Machecoul (see Table III).

Raoul

Girard Chabot III (*d.* 1336). *m.* (1) Jeanne de Parthenay.

Gérard Chabot (*d.* young) *m.* Catherine de Laval.

Jeanne la Folle, *m.* Foulques de Laval (See Table I).

Gérard Chabot IV (*d.* 1344) *m.* Philippe Bertrande de Rouxeville.

Jeanne La Sage (*d.* 1406) adopted Guy de Laval, father of Gilles de Rais.

Gérard Chabot V, "The Posthumous" (*d.* 1351) *m.* Marguerite de Sancerre (No issue).

III. HOUSE OF MACHECOUL.

```
Raoul de Machecoul (d. 1160).
 |
 ├── Bernard.
 ├── Aiméry.
 ├── Oliver I.
 ├── Oliver II (d. 1264).
 ├── Oliver III.
 ├── Gérard, m. Eustachie, d. of Girard Chabot de Rais (see Table II).
 └── Gérard, m. Aliette de Thouars
      |
      ├── Louis, Lord of La Benaste and Le Coustumier, m. Jeanne de Beaucay.
      └── Catherine de Machecoul, m. Pierre de Craon (See Table IV).
           |
           ├── Jean de Craon, m. Béatrice de Rochefort.
           |    |
           |    └── Marie de Craon, m. Guy de Laval, de Rais (See Table I).
           |         |
           |         └── Gilles de Rais (1404-1440).
           └── Pierre and Jeanne (See Table IV).
```

IV. HOUSE OF CRAON.

Renaud I, Count of Nevers, *m.* Adèle of France.
|
Robert de Nevers, Lord of Craon, *m.* Avoise de Sablé.
|
Renaud II, called le Bourguignon.
|
Amaury or Maurice de Craon, *m.* Tiphaine de Champtocé et Ingrandes.
|
├─ Hugues.
├─ Maurice II.
├─ Amaury II.
├─ Maurice IV (?).
├─ Maurice V (?).
├─ Maurice VI (?).
├─ Amaury III, *m.* Béatrice de Roncy, Lady of La Suze.
└─ Pierre de Craon, Lord of La Suze, Ingrandes and Champtocé.
    m. Catherine de Machecoul (See Table III).
    |
    ├─ Pierre (d. 1415 without issue).
    └─ Jean de Craon, Lord of La Suze, etc. *m.* Béatrice de Rochefort.
        |
        ├─ Jeanne, *m.* (1) Ingerger d'Amboise (2) Pierre de Beauvau.
        └─ Marie de Craon, *m.* Guy de Laval, de Rais (see Table I).
            |
            Gilles de Rais (1404-1440).

APPENDIX II

(EXTRACTS FROM THE JUDICIAL CONFESSION OF
GILLES DE RAIS)

IN the presence of the Reverend Father the Lord Bishop of St. Brieuc, of Master Pierre de l'Hôpital the President, Jean de Touscheronde and of Jean Parvai, Gilles de Rais stated on oath that . . . he had stolen or caused to be stolen very many boys—the number he could not remember—that he had put these boys to death and caused them to be killed, and that with them he had committed crimes and sins . . . that he had killed these boys sometimes himself with his own hand, and sometimes through the agency of others, and especially, Gilles de Sillé, Roger de Bricqueville, soldier, Henriet Griart and Corrillaut, *alias* Poitou, Rossignol and little Robin, by various kinds and modes of torture, some by the amputation of their heads from their bodies, using daggers, poignards and knives; others with sticks or other implements for striking, by beating them on the head with violent blows; others again by tying them with cords and fastening them to some door or iron work . . . in his own room that they might be strangled and languish . . . that with these boys even while languishing . . . After their death he took delight in kissing, gazing intently at those who had the more beautifully-formed heads, and in cruelly opening and causing to be opened their bodies that he might see their interior, and that frequently, while these boys were dying, he would sit on their stomachs and take great pleasure in seeing them thus dying, and that he used to laugh heartily at the sight with the said Corrillaut and Griart. The corpses he caused afterwards to be reduced to ashes by the same Corrillaut and Griart and others . . . first he did so in the Château of Champtocé . . . in Machecoul he himself, defendant, seized, killed and caused to be stolen and killed many other boys in large numbers—how many he could not recollect; and again in the Manor of La Suze of Nantes had similarly caused to be killed and burned many other boys, of whom he could not remember the numbers.

Furthermore, he declared and confessed that after the expiration of a year-and-a-half, Eustache Blanchet, aforesaid, summoned the aforesaid François Prelati from the county of Florence in Lombardy and invited him to the same Gilles, defendant, for the purpose of invoking demons, according to the intention of the defendant, and that François informed him that he had discovered in the country whence he came, means of conjuring up a certain spirit by the aid of incantations, which spirit had promised him, François, that he would cause a certain demon called Barron to come to him as the same François might desire. Likewise, the same Gilles de Rais declared and confessed that the said François made several invocations of the demons in compliance with the command of himself. . . . After a certain invocation made by the said François, during the absence of the defendant, the same François, on his return from that very invocation, informed the said defendant that he, François, had seen and addressed the said "Barron" who had told him that he did not appear to the said defendant, because the defendant had deceived him regarding some promises . . . hearing this the said defendant bade François ask the same devil what he wished to receive . . . and that whatever the same "Barron" might wish to receive he, the defendant, would give him, except his soul and life, providing the devil would grant him whatever he would ask. The defendant added that it had been, and was, his intention to ask and acquire from the same devil knowledge, riches and power, by the possession and aid of which he, defendant, would be able to return to his former state of dominion and power, and that afterwards the same François told defendant that he had conversed with the devil and that he among other things required and wished that the defendant present to him the hand, heart, and eyes of a child to be offered and given to the same devil by the said François on the part of the said defendant. . . .

Again the said defendant declared and confessed subsequently that when he was recently at the court of the most illustrious Lord and Prince, the Lord of Brittany, in the Canton Jocelin, of the diocese of Maclovia, he caused to be killed several boys found him by Griart . . . in the above-stated manner . . . and that after the last festival of St. John the Baptist a handsome youth who stayed with a man named Rodigus dwelling in the Place Bourneuf en Rais, was one night brought to him, as he dwelt in the same place, by the same Griart and Corrillaut, and that during the night the defendant . . . caused him to be killed and to be burned near Machecoul. Again at the time of his last stay at Vienne in the month of last July André Buschet delivered over to the said Gilles defendant, in the dwelling-house of a certain Jean Lemoyne a certain boy . . . and that he himself afterwards caused the same Corrillaut to throw the killed lad into the privy of a residence belonging to a certain Boetdan. For which sins and crimes committed by him as stated, he, Gilles de

Rais, accused, humbly and in tears begged mercy and pardon of his Creator and Most Holy Redeemer, as well as the parents and friends of the aforesaid children cruelly murdered and of all others whom he had sinned against or injured.

(*Signed*) DE ALNETO. ⎫
             JO. PARVI. ⎬ *Notaries.*
             G. LESNE. ⎭

APPENDIX III

Extract from Document relating to The Holy Innocents' Foundation

SATURDAY, the twenty-sixth day of March, 1434 (1435, N.S.).
Whereas the noble and powerful Lord, Monseigneur Gilles, Lord of Rais, Count of Grienne, Lord of Champtocé and Pouzages, Marshal of France, did, not long since, for the welfare and salvation of his soul, and in order that his deceased father, mother, relations, friends and benefactors might be held in the memory of Our Lord Jesus Christ, make a Foundation in memory of the Holy Innocents at the spot called Machecoul en Rais, which is in the Duchy of Brittany; whereas in this said Foundation, he did make and ordain a Curate, Dean, Archdeacon, treasmen, canons, chaplains and college, and did order and provide revenues and possessions for their livelihood and necessaries . . . and whereas the said Lord did and still has a full intention and firm resolve to maintain the said Foundation as he has shown and does each day show by his

deeds, now he, desiring with all his heart that the said Curate, Dean and Chapter shall, after his death, remain in good and peaceful possession of the revenues and possessions thus assigned to them, and shall be preserved and defended from all oppression, hath given first the Castle and Castellany of Champtocé to the King of Sicily and Duke of Anjou, from whom they are held in brief; and secondly, one half of all the lordship, barony, and land of Rais to the Duke of Brittany in order of Madame Catherine de Thouars, wife of the said Monseigneur de Rais or Mademoiselle Marie de Rais, his daughter, or any other relatives, friends, heirs, or claimants . . . should, by whatever title or manner or for whatever cause, deny and prevent the said Foundation, then that day, the said Lords, the King of Sicily, and Duke of Angou and the Duke of Brittany, shall help, sustain, and defend the members of the said Foundation in order that they may enjoy it fully and peacefully.

Considering that neither he (Gilles) nor any other human creature can requite his Creator for the benefits derived from His grace and benevolence, and that it is a necessary thing to acquire an intercessor, by the help of whom one may, in continuation of temporal welfare, attain to the glory of spiritual prosperity.

APPENDIX IV

THE LEGEND OF BLUEBEARD

THROUGHOUT Lower Brittany and the Vendée, popular tradition persists in regarding Gilles de Rais as the original Bluebeard. He is never referred to as other than the *Barbe Bleue*, and the old legend is identical in its French setting. The peasants round Tiffauges will tell you with all seriousness that the wife of the wicked *Barbe Bleue* who lived in the Château one day peeped into the secret chamber and saw seven heads of her predecessors. With her sister she mounted to the tower of the donjon to look for succour:

" *Anne, ma sœur Anne, ne vois-tu rien venir ?*"
" *Je vois le chemin qui poudroie et l'herbe qui verdoie.*"

There is another more poetical native account which relates how Messire Gilles de Rais, tired of warring against the English, retired to Tiffauges, where all his time was spent in carousals and pleasuring. One night there passed his castle, going to Morlaix, a cavalier, the Count Odon de Tremeac, Lord of Krevent and other places. The young *seigneur* was accompanied by Blanche de l'Herminière, a beautiful young maiden to whom he was affianced. The Lord of Tiffauges invited the couple to rest at the Château and drink a goblet of hypocras with him. The travellers were anxious to go their way, but de Rais showed himself so pressing and so amiable that they consented to partake of his hospitality.

After an interval they rose to pursue their journey, but the *Barbe Bleue* made some excuse to detain them, and so induced them to stay until night had fallen. Suddenly, on a sign from the master of the Château, a body of archers marched into the banqueting hall, seized the Count de Tremeac and threw him into the deep pit. De Rais begged the lady to forgive this trifling discourtesy and accept him as a substitute for the hapless Count. Blanche wept abundantly and indignantly refused to be pacified. De Rais brushed aside her opposition and her tears and dragged her to the chapel, intending to wed her forcibly forthwith. A thousand candles glowed on the altar, and the bells rang a nuptial peal. "Quick, sir Chaplain, marry us," cried the impetuous wooer.

"I do not want my Lord as spouse," the maid protested. and turned to flee.

The *Barbe Bleue* seized her and again led her to the altar. "I will give you everything," declared he, passionately, "the most beautiful gems and ornaments, my castles, woods, fields and meadows belong to you. I give you my body and soul."

At this declaration a change came over the fair Blanche.

"I accept, I accept," she exclaimed. "Do you hear me, Gilles de Rais, Lord of Tiffauges? Henceforth you belong to me." At the same instant the beautiful Blanche became an azure-blue devil, who addressed the *Barbe Bleue* in a voice like thunder.

"Gilles de Rais," said the devil with a sinister laugh, "God is tired of your misdeeds. You belong now to Hell, and from this moment you have put on its livery."

As he uttered these words, the devil made a sign, and de Rais' beard, which till then was auburn, became blue-black.

"You will not be Gilles de Rais any longer," said the devil, "you will be the *Barbe Bleue*, the most frightful of men and the terror of women and children. Your name will be accursed for all ages, and after death your ashes will be cast upon the winds, whilst your ugly soul shall go down to the depth of Hell."

De Rais begged for mercy, but the demon only laughed and spoke of the corpses of the seven wives which lay in the caverns of the castle. "The Lord Odon de Tremeac, whom I rode with under the guise of Blanche de l'Herminière, is at this moment at the head of a band of knights in your pursuit. They will avenge all your murders."

"Alas, I am lost!" cried de Rais.

"Not yet," answered the devil, "for I have need of you. Alive you will serve me a thousand times better than dead, and now till our next meeting."

With this parting shot the devil disappeared in a cloud of sulphur.

It is further related that the devil kept his word, and prevented the intervention of Count Odon, but from that moment Gilles de Rais became the *Barbe Bleue* of history. An even older Breton legend, dating from the sixth century, bears a curious resemblance to the *Barbe Bleue* story. The hero is Comor, an Arthurian prince, and the heroine the daughter of Guerole, count of Vannes. She is beheaded by her husband, who had previously slain four wives. His last victim is brought to life again by Saint Gildas. Comor, like Gilles, was cursed and excommunicated by a council of Bishops.

Hernandez gives an interesting sidelight on the tradition that the original Bluebeard was a native of Brittany. In 1890 a scientific expedition landed at Vanikoro, an island in the South Seas, and incidentally discovered a local legend called "Papalacatza," *i.e.*, blue flame, which bore a suspicious resemblance to the old nursery story. On inquiry they were told that it had originally been brought to Vanikoro by a sailor from Nantes who, owing to one of the native girls falling in love with him, had escaped being massacred. He learned Polynesian and related to his children the story of the *Barbe Bleue* as told him by his mother, who had heard it from her own mother, a native of Machecoul.

APPENDIX V

MSS. DOCUMENTS OF THE TRIALS

THE original account of the Canonical Trial, drawn up in Latin, is found in the Archives of the Loire Inférieure (No. 9175) as is also the *Mémoire des Héritiers* (No. 9189). There is a facsimile of the first sixteen pages in the Public Library of Nantes (Latin 89) and a few other copies are scattered throughout the country.

A copy was given to the Sires de la Tremoille, whose descendants have preserved the documents.

A copy is also extant in the Library of Carpentras.

The Public Library of Nantes possesses a modernized copy (Latin 124).

Two more are to be found in the National Library in Paris. From the first MSS. (Latin 17663) is taken one of the miniatures reproduced. The second MS. (French 21395) was collated under the Second Empire upon the original manuscript. It was certified to be identical with the original by M. Louis Paris, director of the Historical Cabinet.

What is considered to be the original account of the Civil Trial is a copy of the notes of the Trial, made in 1530 at the request of Gilles de Laval and his wife Françoise de Maille under the eyes of Gilles de Rouge, Knight and Councillor-in-ordinary to the King of France and other people. It figures amongst the communal archives of Thouars.

A copy made directly from the Thouars manuscript is found in the Nantes Library (French 1882), which also possesses another (French 1881) made from a manuscript in the National Library.

The Nantes Library contains two other manuscripts bearing upon the subject; one (French 1883) is the *Réclamation des héritiers de Rais*—against the confiscation of the Marshal's goods. The other (French 1886) is a copy of the authentic report of the accusation.

The National Archives possess two accounts of the Civil Trial, written in French.

APPENDIX VI

LIST OF WORKS CONSULTED

Alain Bouchart: *Les Grandes Croniques de Bretagne.* 1514.

D'Argentre: *Histoire de Bretagne.* 1558.

Du Paz: *Histoire généalogique de plusieurs illustres maisons de Bretagne.* 1620.

Guillaume Gruel: *Histoire d'Artus III, Duc de Bretagne.* 1622.

Mezeray: *Histoire de France.* 1643.

Jean Chartier: *Histoire de Charles VII.* 1661.

Dom Lobineau: *Histoire de la Bretagne.* 1707.

Montfaucon: *Monuments de la Monarchie française.* 1729.

Voltaire: *Essai sur les mœurs.* 1756.

Des Essarts: *Procès fameux.* 1788.

Michel Guimar: *Annales nantaises.* 1795.

Dom Morice: *MSS. de Nantes.* 1808.

Ed. Richer : *Description des bords d'Erdre.* 1820.

J. F. Bodin : *Recherches historiques sur l'Anjou.* 1821.

De Roujoux : *Histoire des Rois et des Ducs de Bretagne.* 1828.

Pitre-Chevalier : *La Bretagne ancienne et moderne.* 1844.

Mourain de Sourdaval : *Les Seigneurs de Rais.* 1845.

Vallet de Viriville : *Notices et extraits de Chartes et de Manuscrits appartenant au British Museum.* (Bibl. de l'Ec. des Chartes, VIII). 1846.

Armand Guéraud : *Notice sur Gilles de Rais.* 1855.

Douet-D'Arcq : *Edition de la Chronique de Monstrelet.* 1857.

P. Marchegay : *Revue des Provinces de l'Ouest.* (T.V. p. 177). 1857.

P. L. Jacob : *Curiosités de l'histoire de France, 2e série.* 1858.

Guillaume Couginot : *Chronique de la Pucelle.* 1859.

Morel : *La folie héréditaire (Gazette Hebdomadaire).* 1861.

Vallet de Viriville : *Histoire de Charles VII.* 1862.

Vallet de Viriville : *Nouvelle Biogr. Génér. Didot.* 1866.

P. Wallon : *Revue des questions historiques.* 1871.

P. Marchegay : *Notices et pièces historiques sur l'Anjou*, etc. 1772.

Célestin Post : *Dictionnaire du Maine-et-Loire.* 1874.

P. Marchegay : *Documents relatifs à Prégent de Coëtivy.* 1876.

Charles Deulin : *Les Contes de ma mère l'Oye avant Perrault.* 1878.

Jules Michelet : *Histoire de France.* 1885.

Abbé Bossard : *Gilles de Rais.* 1885.

Abbé Bossard *et* René de Maulde : *Gilles de Rais.* 1886.

Ch. Lemire : *La Barbe Bleue de la Légende et de l'Histoire.* 1886.

Moll : *Les Perversions de l'instinct génital.* 1893.

Krafft-Ebing : *Psychopathia Sexualis.* 1895.

Blanchard : *Cartulaire des Sires de Rays (Archives historiques de Poitou).* 1898.

Thoinot : *Attentats aux mœurs et perversions du sens génital.* 1898.

J. K. Huysmans : *Gilles de Rais. La Magie en Poitou.* 1899.

Petit-Dutaillis : *Histoire de France de Michelet.* 1901.

Ch. Lea : *Histoire de l'Inquisition au Moyen-Age,* translated by Salomon Reinach. 1902.

Salomon Reinach : *L'Anjou historique.* March, 1902.

Jean Holp: *Eveils d'automne. Chez Barbe-Bleue* (*Le Signal*, October 16). 1902.

Salomon Reinach: (*Le Signal*, October 21). 1902.

Salomon Reinach: (*Revue des Universités de Belgique*, December). 1904.

Salomon Reinach: (*Comptes rendus de l'Académie des Inscriptions et Belles-Lettres*, Session of January 13). 1905.

Marcel Baudouin: *Intermédiaire des Chercheurs et des Curieux*. 1905.

Marcel Baudouin: (*Intermédiaire Nantais*, January 26). 1906.

Arthur le Moyne de la Borderie: *Histoire de Bretagne*. 1906.

F. H. Bernelle: *La Psychose de Gilles de Rays*. 1910.

Salomon Reinach: *Cultes, Mythes et Religions*. 1912.

de Cabanes: *Légendes et Curiosités de l'Histoire, 1re serie*. 1912.

Salomon Reinach: (*Revue Archéologique*, p. 447). 1913.

Noel Vallois: *Le Procès de Gilles de Rais*. 1913.

Ch. V. Langlois: *Notice sur M. Noel Vallois* (*Comptes rendus de l'Académie des Inscriptions et Belles-Lettres*). 1918.

Funck-Brentano: *La véritable histoire de Barbe-Bleue* (*Mes Loisirs*, July 15). 1919.

Funck-Brentano: *Brigands et Routiers.* 1919.

P. Saintyves: *Barbe-Bleue: Essai de Folklore et d'Ethnographie.* 1921.

Elie Richard: *La Constance du Satanisme* (*Mercure de France*, November 1). 1921.

BRISTOL : BURLEIGH LTD.
AT THE BURLEIGH PRESS

CPSIA information can be obtained at www.ICGtesting.com
Printed in the USA
BVOW03s1451080414

350076BV00021B/1335/P